DEAR BOB, DEAR BETTY: LOVE AND MARRIAGE DURING THE GREAT DEPRESSION

DEAR BOB, DEAR BETTY: LOVE AND MARRIAGE DURING THE GREAT DEPRESSION

THE COURTSHIP LETTERS OF ROBERT LLEWELLYN WRIGHT AND ELIZABETH BRYAN KEHLER, OCTOBER 1932–AUGUST 1933

Transcriptions, Annotations, Foreword, and Introduction
by

Elizabeth Catherine Wright

ISBN 978-0-557-06457-1
LCCN 2009904257

ACKNOWLEDGMENTS

I wish to thank the following people for their assistance with my archival research:

Indira Berndtson, Administrator, Historic Studies, The Frank Lloyd Wright Foundation Archives at Taliesin West, Scottsdale, Arizona.

Keith Bringe, former Executive Director of the Unity Temple Restoration Foundation, Oak Park, Illinois.

Meg Diaz, former Director of Advancement at Milwaukee Technical College, Milwaukee, Wisconsin.

Ciaran Escoffery, Director of Alumni Relations, Francis W. Parker School, Chicago, Illinois.

Andy Kaplan, Archivist at Francis W. Parker School, Chicago, Illinois.

Patricia Leavy, Manager, Nineteenth Century Club, Oak Park, Illinois.

Frank Lipo, Executive Director of the Historical Society of Oak Park and River Forest, Oak Park, Illinois.

Sally McKay and the staff of the Reference Library at the Getty Center, Los Angeles, California.

Tim Samuelson, Cultural Historian for the City of Chicago, Chicago, Illinois.

Marilyn Thomas, Director of the Office of Public Relations, John Marshall Law School, Chicago, Illinois.

Don Vogel, Archivist, Oak Park and River Forest High School, Oak Park, Illinois.

For their help and encouragement during the research, writing, and publication process, I am most grateful to the following people:

Jean-Charles Belliard, Angiola Bonanni, Laura Bresler, Keith Bringe, Adrian Burns, Katy McDowell Brooks, Camille Cusumano, Sheila Dolan, Maxine Gold, Nancy Horan, Libby Jordan, Maura McDowell Kealey, Myra Kaplan, Leslie Lauderdale, Judy Barrett Litoff, Casey Llewellyn, the staff at Lulu Press, Martha and John Lunz, Malcolm Margolin, James Marten, the Potluck Players, Amelia Ray, Edie Smith, Bruce Tippett, Donna Weidenfeller, Dave Wilson, and Timothy Kehler Wright.

I dedicate this publication to my parents, with much affection.

FOREWORD

I first discovered these letters in August 2003, while clearing out my mother's belongings from her house, after her senile dementia had already reached an advanced stage. They were carefully filed away in a cardboard box in one of the dresser drawers in my mother's bedroom, in the home to which she would never return. As I started reading through them, I was fascinated to see unfolding before my eyes the story of the intense nine-month courtship that had preceded their marriage. I was astonished to see my father expressing so much emotion, something I had rarely experienced from him, and amazed at how well written the letters were, as both parties clearly pulled out all the stops to impress each other. At the same time, they were genuinely trying to figure out a way to join together in married life without undue financial hardship during the depths of the great economic Depression, 1932–33.

Although I knew some of the story of their marriage, I had never seen them express love so directly to each other the way they did in the letters. When I was growing up, my view of their relationship was not a positive one. My father was often absent, and when he was there, I saw my mother nagging him, and him turning away from her. My father also rarely expressed his feelings directly to anyone. He would tell my mother how much he loved me, and tell me how much he cared for her, but neither of us heard it directly from him. When he became immobilized from the progression of congestive heart failure and needed constant care during the last two years of his life, she devoted herself to him unflaggingly, and I began to glimpse how much they appreciated each other. My father even began to realize shortly before his death in February 1986 that he needed to express his feelings more directly, though it was too late in his life for him to make any great changes in this regard.

I began to read the letters aloud to my mother during my visits to her at the nursing home. I was delighted when she occasionally smiled at certain events evoked in the letters, because she was generally quite withdrawn during that period, often completely silent and unexpressive despite my attempts to amuse and interest her. I was never able to get any more reaction or information out of her concerning the letters, and she died a couple of years later in November of 2005.

Thus I was never able to discuss the letters directly with either of my parents, but finding their correspondence has led me to explore their lives further, in order to understand the circumstances that formed who they were at the time of the courtship and afterwards.

For my mother's life, I have drawn heavily on the video interviews my brother Tim conducted with her in July 1989, while her memory was still relatively good, where she talked extensively about her early life before meeting my father, as well as their courtship and her subsequent life with him.

For my father's life, I have used a series of essays he wrote in the form of letters to his children, as well as letters between him and his father, Frank Lloyd Wright, before and during the period of the courtship, preserved in the Frank Lloyd Wright archive. I have also drawn information from the numerous published works exploring his father's family life.

I gained additional insights from a pilgrimage I made to Chicago and Milwaukee in October 2005 to visit the sites of the addresses contained in the letters, accompanied by my brother Tim and his daughter Casey, who documented on film the areas we visited. We went to North Sixth and West State Streets, the location of the Milwaukee Vocational School where my mother had worked, and toured the original building still standing as part of the Milwaukee Area Technical College. We drove to her home address on 1834 North Prospect Avenue in Milwaukee, now a parking lot for a nursing home, which still provides an idea of the lovely lakeshore view she must have had from her apartment. We searched in vain for my father's office building in Chicago, 110 Dearborn Street, which no longer exists. I later learned that it was the old Westminster Building, documented in postcards and directories from the period. His home address in Chicago's fancy near North Side, 63 East Division Street, also no longer exists, but nearby apartments allowed us to envision the basement apartment where he lived at the time, and into which my parents moved after they were married.

We were able to visit the family home where my father grew up in Oak Park, Illinois, now open to the public as the Frank Lloyd Wright Home and Studio. We visited Oak Park High School, which my father attended for ninth and tenth grades, The Francis W. Parker School in Chicago, where he completed his junior and senior years of high school, and John Marshall Law School, where he earned his JD after attending at night from 1927–30. We rode the train between Milwaukee and Chicago as my parents had done, though the electric trains of their time that connected directly with the electric L in Chicago no longer exist.

Additional research at the Chicago and Milwaukee public libraries during a second visit in July 2006 provided me with documentation about some of the public events my parents mention in the letters—bank closings, blizzards, the 1933 World's Fair, reviews of plays they attended and books they read. On a third visit to Oak Park and Chicago in July 2008, I found more information about my mother's family in the archives of the Oak Park Historical Society, and in the Chicago city directories housed in the Newberry Library. I was able to visit the house my maternal grandmother purchased when she first moved to Oak Park, where my mother was probably born, and also view the exterior of the house on the south side of the tracks in Oak Park, where she spent her early childhood.

My brother and niece shot video footage during the first of these trips, which my brother is editing into a documentary about courtship then and now. However, it is the language of the letters and the story they tell that have most interested me and have motivated me to transcribe and edit them in order to make them available to a larger public. Work on this publication has been a voyage of discovery for me, and a labor of love, as I have come to understand the deep emotional bond my parents formed during their courtship that continued to nourish them throughout their lives. I address this book to them with great affection, as a way to honor their love for each other.

Contents

Introduction

In the fall of 1909, Frank Lloyd Wright left his wife, Catherine Tobin Wright, and six children in Oak Park, Illinois, to sail to Europe with Mamah Borthwick Cheney, a client of his who also left her husband and children behind in Oak Park. Robert Llewellyn Wright, the youngest of the six children, was five years old at the time of his father's departure.[1]

Several months later, between April and July 1910, James Howard Kehler, a prominent Chicago advertising man who was a friend of Wright's, deserted his wife, Elizabeth Osgood Kehler, and their two young sons to marry Keith Ransom, a widow with a young daughter to whom he had rented a cottage on the Kehlers' residence in Deerfield, Illinois. Elizabeth Bryan Kehler, born in Oak Park on July 21, 1910, was still in the womb at the time of her father's abandonment of the family.[2]

---

[1] Meryle Secrest, *Frank Lloyd Wright* (New York: Alfred A. Knopf, 1992), 187–203. RLW was called Llewellyn by his family, and Bob by his friends later in life. Born on November 15, 1903, he turned six about a month after his father's departure.

[2] EBK was called Betty by her family and friends. The information about her life in this Introduction comes from her videotaped memoirs unless otherwise stated. The 1910 census, dated April 18, shows James H. Kehler and Elizabeth N. Kehler (perhaps a misprint for Elizabeth M. Kehler—her maiden name was Elizabeth May Osgood) living as husband and wife with their two sons, Gordon M. and Stuart W., in West Deerfield, Lake County, Illinois (Year: 1910; Census Place: West Deerfield, Lake, Illinois; Roll: T624_302; Page: 3A; Enumeration District: 120; Image: 590). However, the 1910–11 Oak Park Directory (p. 139) shows Mrs. Elizabeth Osgood Kehler living at 119 N. Kenilworth Avenue in Oak Park. Thus she must have left the Deerfield residence and moved to Oak Park sometime after April 18, 1910, the census date, and before Betty's birth, in Oak Park, on July 21, 1910. The 1920 census shows James H. Kehler and Keith R. Kehler as lodgers at the same address in Chicago (Year: 1920; Census Place: Chicago Ward 21, Cook [Chicago], Illinois; Roll: T625_332; Page: 17A; Enumeration District: 1189; Image: 423).

1. *James Howard Kehler*

Frank Lloyd Wright and James Howard Kehler had much in common. They were both innovators in their respective artistic fields, and probably traded Japanese prints with each other during the period when Kehler had an office in the Fine Arts Building in Chicago, from 1903 to 1915. Both were known for their flamboyance and charisma, and both were members of the Cliff Dwellers Club, a society formed to encourage Chicago artists.[3]

While Frank Lloyd Wright returned briefly to the family home in 1910, by October of 1911 he was living with Mamah Borthwick on his mother's family land in Hillside, Wisconsin, in the first of the residences he called Taliesin.

---

3 A letter from Llewellyn to his father dated Jan. 31, 1933, announcing his engagement to Betty (W067B07 in the Frank Lloyd Wright archive) says, "I believe you used to trade Japanese prints with her father, James Howard Kehler, when he had an office the Fine Arts Building." Wright's reply to Llewellyn from Spring Green, Wisconsin, dated Feb. 15 (W067C09) mentions "my friend Jim Kehler...." The Chicago City Directories show Kehler having an office in the Fine Arts Building continuously from 1904 to 1915, and Wright having an office there in 1908. An obituary for Kehler written by a member of the Cliff Dwellers Club (identified only as C.C.) bears out Betty's description of her father, and describes him in a manner that does echo many descriptions of Wright at the time. See the Appendix for a full transcription of this obituary.

Catherine Tobin Wright remained in the family house in Oak Park and refused to give her husband a divorce for over ten years.[4] She finally gave in, and the divorce decree was signed and settled on November 13, 1922, shortly before Llewellyn's nineteenth birthday.[5] Llewellyn was thus brought up solely by his mother, with occasional visits to his father, and some financial support from him.[6]

---

4 Secrest, 205–12. Wright's tumultuous love life and financial dealings, and their effect on his family, are evocatively portrayed in two recent works of historical fiction, Nancy Horan's *Loving Frank* (New York: Ballantine Books, Random House, 2007), and T. C. Boyle's *The Women* (London: Bloomsbury, 2009). William R. Drennan's *Death in a Prairie House: Frank Lloyd Wright and the Taliesin Murders* (Madison, WI: Terrace Books/U of Wisconsin Press, 2007) is a dramatic historical investigation of the murder of Mamah, her children, and others residing at Taliesin in 1914.

5 Secrest, 271. While divorce was still rare in the United States in the early twentieth century, the rate was multiplying, growing from 1.5 per 1,000 marriages in 1870 to 7.7 per 1,000 in 1920 (Paul H. Jacobson, *American Marriage and Divorce* [New York, 1959], pp. 21, 90, table reproduced in *Great Expectations, Marriage and Divorce in Post-Victorian America* by Elaine Tyler May [Chicago and London: U of Chicago Press, 1980], 167). Betty's brother Stewart, who introduced her to Llewellyn, married a divorcee shortly before Betty and Bob were married (Letter No. 123).

6 Llewellyn left home to attend Cornell University in 1921 but still lived intermittently with his mother until she married Ben Page, in June of 1930. This coincided with Llewellyn's graduation from law school and the start of his work for the Chicago firm of Mayer, Meyer, Austrian, and Platt (see below in this Introduction). Page was a widower and retired Chicago businessman, who had helped Frank Lloyd Wright with his financial problems in 1928 and by 1930 had assumed the position of treasurer of the corporation founded to handle Wright's finances. At that time he had recently bought Speedwell Farm, a historic property in Illinois' corn belt. Page, however, soon lost his wealth due to the stock market crash and some poor investments, and was dropped from Wright's inner circle. Catherine eventually found their tastes incompatible, said she did not enjoy the isolated farm life, and moved back into Chicago. The Pages were divorced in 1937 (Secrest, 342; 359–61). At the time of the courtship letters in 1932-33, Catherine is living in Gary, Indiana, probably with Page. A card from Catherine to Llewellyn dated Dec. 4 1932, has the letterhead Catherine L. Page, 202 West 45th Avenue, Gary, Indiana, and another undated letter from her to Llewellyn found with the courtship correspondence invites him to bring Betty to dinner at Gary on March 26, to celebrate her own and "Pesh's" birthday (undated letter between Letters No. 57 and 58. Bob mentions going to visit his mother in Gary in Letter No. 11; Betty refers to the March 26 visit in Letter No. 63).

2. *Catherine Tobin Wright*

Elizabeth Osgood Kehler, in contrast to Catherine Tobin Wright, left the Deerfield residence she shared with her husband and moved to Oak Park before her daughter was born.[7] Two years later, in 1912, she married a widowed real estate agent, William R. Lloyd, who sold her the first house she lived in there. After their marriage, the Lloyds and Elizabeth's children lived in a large house on the south side of Oak Park until Betty was about eight years old. Her mother joined the Oak Park Nineteenth Century Woman's Club in November 1911, where Catherine Tobin Wright was already an active member.[8]

[7] See n. 2.

[8] The handwritten Vice President's Report dated Apr. 22, 1912, lists "Elizabeth Kehler" as one of the new members "added to our numbers this year [1911–12]" (pp. 3–4). The 1912–13 printed calendar of the club, however, with members' names and addresses, shows Elizabeth Lloyd as a member inducted in Nov. 1911, with the address Mrs. William R. Lloyd, 422 Clinton Avenue, Oak Park. This will remain the same through the 1916–17 calendar. Her marriage to Wm. R. Lloyd thus must have

3. Elizabeth Osgood Kehler

Betty had positive memories of her early years in Oak Park. She remembered her mother as happy when she was newly remarried and had money, and she recalled fondly how her stepfather used to take her for Sunday walks to admire the Frank Lloyd Wright houses, including the home and studio where Llewellyn grew up.

---

taken place in 1912, sometime after April 22 of that year, and prior to the publication of the club's 1912–13 calendar. I thank Frank Lipo of the Historical Society of Oak Park and River Forest for guiding me to these materials housed in their collection. Frank Lloyd Wright's mother Anna was a founding member of the club; Mamah Borthwick Cheney and Catherine Tobin Wright were members from 1903 on (Secrest, 225; 193). *The Gentle Force: A History of the Nineteenth Century Woman's Club of Oak Park* by Carolyn O. Poplett with Mary Ann Porucznik (Broadview, IL: A. & H. Lithoprint, 1988, 1992) is a good general guide to the club, and I thank the club manager, Patricia Leavy, for presenting me with a copy on my visit in 2008.

4. 422 Clinton Avenue, Oak Park, IL, c. 1912. Residence of William R. Lloyd and Elizabeth Osgood Kehler Lloyd, where Betty grew up.

5. Betty in Oak Park, 1912

6. Betty and her mother

Llewellyn's early years were more difficult. His letters to his father in the first years after the departure reveal a very tender young boy who misses his father greatly.[9] In his memoirs, written later in life in the form of letters to his children, he recounts:

[9] On Oct. 21, 1911, Llewellyn writes his father in Hillside, Wisconsin: "dear papa how are you I am feeling sad with out you I love you very much.... I like my music lessons I want to play like you some day. ... these are good night kisses ooooooooo from your loving little boy...." On his eighth birthday of the same year, Nov. 15, 1911, Llewellyn writes: "Dear Papa This is my birthday. I miss you very much. Will you please eat Thanksgiving dinner with us. We are lonesome with out you. We are afraid you are sick. .... I am eight years old. good bye from your loving son". On the last page he puts eight "birthday kisses oooooooo." Excerpted from Llewellyn Wright to Frank Lloyd Wright, W016B09 and W023A01, in the Frank Lloyd Wright Archive, Copyright, The Frank Lloyd Wright Foundation 1990. Other undated letters from Llewellyn to his father copied on the W023 fiche, clearly written when he was a young boy, express similar sentiments. While it is quite likely that his mother was encouraging Llewellyn to write letters such as these as part of her strategy to win Frank back, the handwriting and forms of expression are clearly those of a child, and the emotion in them comes across as quite genuine.

> The only small child memory of my father that has stayed with me was the final departure. My tearful mother held my hand while my cheerful father waved goodbye to us in the fall of 1909. Why my mother was crying and my father smiling I did not understand. Mrs. Cheney's name had not then been heard by me. I understand now and I don't believe he was quite as happy as he seemed. He had a lifelong habit of covering miserable situations with a bright smile.[10]

7. Llewellyn Wright at age six, 1909

Subsequent letters from Llewellyn to his father, as he grew older, often contain pleas for clothes and money and other gifts, and some are thank-you notes to his father for what he does receive.[11] Though these demonstrate that he obviously desired his father's generosity, Llewellyn later recalled deploring his father's indebtedness.

> I remember visiting him in his Chicago hotel room when I was about twelve ... and seeing him stave off an insistent creditor with jocular excuses. When the man left, he turned to me, all smiles, and said 'Son, that's the way you handle creditors.' I didn't think so then and still don't.

---

[10] Robert Llewellyn Wright, unpublished letters to his children, "Your Father's Recollections of His Father." Llewellyn in a later essay reflecting on reading the Ashbee papers felt this "final departure" scene might have instead taken place in 1910 or 1911.

[11] Frank Lloyd Wright Archive, Llewellyn Wright to Frank Lloyd Wright, other undated letters with the W023 prefix, clearly written when Llewellyn was still quite young, as well as W041A10 (01/01/20), W043A04 (02/04/21), and W045D07 (01/27/29).

To me he had just gone through such a humiliating experience that I have been afraid to buy anything on credit ever since.[12]

The public scandals concerning his father's private life were also a source of shame to Llewellyn as an adolescent. The press treatment of his father's career and life "was a terrible embarrassment during my high school days in Oak Park. At that time my father was more notorious than famous.... [B]eing his son was no honor in the community."[13]

Betty's happy life with her mother and stepfather changed after they left Oak Park when she was around eight years old, in 1918. Her stepfather felt called to become a Congregational minister, and took his wife and adopted daughter with him to a series of small Midwestern towns where he found parishes to hire him. Although Betty loved the rural farm life she experienced during this period, her stepfather's ministerial career was never very successful, and Betty felt that her mother resented the duties she had to take on as a minister's wife. Rather than complain to her husband, her mother retreated into illness, suffering mild nervous breakdowns and becoming a semi-invalid.

Betty, who had loved "Daddy Lloyd" when she was young, as a teenager chafed at the restrictions her stepfather placed on her, and hated having to conform to the expectations for a minister's daughter in a small town. She was reproached for such things as skipping rather than walking down the street, and began to rebel by taking up smoking and hanging out with a group of tough kids. At the same time, her mother's cousin Annie, who lived with the family and did all the cooking, had a stroke. Because Betty's mother, who was already ill, then had to take care of cousin Annie, Betty was asked to take over all the cooking and housework chores. Daddy Lloyd, who had previously helped Betty's mother with the housework due to her illness, offered no such help to Betty, and she resented having to take on all these chores with no help at the age of twelve.

---

[12] Unpublished letters to his children, "Your Father's Recollection of His Father." Llewellyn in fact did avoid debt all his life. The concern he expressed in his courtship letters to his future wife Betty, about building up enough savings to sustain the marriage, and his complete honesty with her about his financial situation, were no doubt related to his desire to avoid the path of his father, who continually lived beyond his means and fended off creditors all his life.

[13] Ibid. Llewellyn attended Oak Park High School from 1917–19, and then transferred to The Francis W. Parker School in Chicago from 1919–21. Records from the latter school show a Chicago address on Division Street for him, very likely the address of an apartment he shared with his mother at the time.

8. Wm. R. Lloyd (driving), l. to r.: his sister Zilpha, Betty, cousin Annie

9. Postcard of Congregational Church and parsonage, St. Charles, Minnesota, one of the parishes to which Wm. R. Lloyd took his family

Although her stepfather thoroughly disapproved of Betty's real father, her mother insisted she be allowed contact with him. Betty saw James occasionally in Oak Park during the early years, and then after she moved away with her mother and stepfather, she spent several weeks with him and his new family each summer at the Deerfield property. She idolized him, and found him much more interesting than her stepfather. He developed heart trouble, however, and died in 1923, shortly before Betty's thirteenth birthday. Her stepfather, who thoroughly disapproved of Kehler, had forbidden her to mention that she had any father other than himself, and this was particularly painful for Betty when her father died. She tried to confide her sadness at this event to a friend, who could not even understand what Betty meant.

Betty thus suffered under the restricted life she lived with her stepfather, while adoring and admiring from afar her unconventional father, who was absent from her daily life and unknown to her friends. Llewellyn, by contrast, suffered from the public notoriety of his father and in general desired to pursue a more ordinary life. When it was time for him to go to college, he rejected his father's "appalling suggestion that I go to China to study with a philosopher friend of his. An education was to me a way of fitting into a conventional, orderly career."[14] His father yielded, and paid the bills for Llewellyn's three and half years at Cornell University plus a summer school session at the University of Wisconsin in Madison to complete the BA degree in economics in 1925.

After graduation, however, he had neither a clear career goal nor much desire to work. He had obtained the conventional education he desired, but found it rather uninspiring: "I had become very tired of education and felt over-educated. After enrolling in 1921 as a five year civil engineering student I had shifted to Arts and Sciences to get it over with in four years. This I managed in three and one half, with a University of Wisconsin summer session. But I didn't know what to do next."[15]

For a couple of years, he worked at a number of different jobs, none of them satisfactory to him, alternating with periods of leisure living off his mother, who was employed and always gave him "a place to eat and sleep." Finally, while working as an insurance adjuster, he "quickly learned that all adjusters enrolled in night law school if they wanted to progress." He went to John Marshall Law School in Chicago as a night student from 1927 to 1930, found it "easy," and thus began his lifelong career as a lawyer.[16]

When it came time for Betty to go to college, she experienced a family conflict of a different sort than Llewellyn's. After her father's death, her brother Gordon, ten years older than she, had assumed the paternal role and paid for her to go to a girls' boarding school, Monticello Seminary in Alton, Illinois. The idea was to prepare her for Vassar College, the alma mater of Keith Ransom and her

---

14 Ibid., "Your Father's Recollection of His Father."

15 Ibid., "Not Making It in the Twenties."

16 Ibid.

daughter Julia. However, after Betty completed this boarding school education, which she hated and found even more repressive than life with her stepfather, she was told at the last minute that she could not go to Vassar. Instead she was to attend the University of Wisconsin at Madison, where her mother and stepfather were then living. Betty never understood why the plan was changed. There may have been financial issues, but her brother Gordon said it was her mother's decision, and one can imagine that neither her mother nor her stepfather were eager to have Betty follow in the footsteps of the woman for whom James had abandoned his family.

10. Julia Ransom, during her Vassar days

Betty was crushed at the time about not going to Vassar, but later was glad she had attended a coed university. She enrolled there from 1927–31, and was an excellent student, earning Phi Beta Kappa in her junior year. She also enjoyed the social life there, both the opportunity to mingle with men, and the lifelong friendships she made with other women through living in the Sigma Kappa sorority house.

She finished college with a degree in economic statistics in 1931, and Llewellyn and she later discovered they had studied economics with the same professor. Graduating in the middle of the Depression made it difficult for Betty to find a job, but she did manage to obtain one as a receptionist for a group of counselors at the Milwaukee Vocational School. She got the position through a college friend, Margaret Cooley, the daughter of the school's principal and founder R. L. Cooley.

11. Betty in April 1931, the year she graduated from college

Llewellyn, who had graduated from law school in 1930, worked from 1930–32 in the Chicago firm of Mayer, Meyer, Austrian, and Platt,[17] and in 1932, when he met Betty, he had just launched a private practice.

According to their accounts, neither of them had had any satisfactory romantic experiences before they met in the fall of 1932.

In his memoirs, Llewellyn writes about "the girls of Oak Park" and other women he met later on in life. In Oak Park, none of the girls he admired were interested in him, and he also recounts two failed experiences in 1931 with young women who rejected him. One was rich and felt he wasn't treating her with enough deference; the other was a dairy farmer's daughter working at a dime-a-dance hall, whom he thought he could introduce to his world of "middle class

[17] Alumni Directory, John Marshall Law School, Class of 1930.

pretensions." She accepted his invitation to see a play, but when he arrived with the tickets at the address she had given him, no one answered the door.[18]

Betty said that she was restricted from any real contact with boys as a teenager, both while living with her minister stepfather and at the boarding school she attended. At the University of Wisconsin, she was pleased to have more contact with men, but found the college boys of her age rather juvenile. One of them asked her to marry him, but she had no interest in him. She said she was too brainy to be popular, didn't have many dates, and was convinced she was not attractive and would never marry. Her male models were her father and her brothers, eight and ten years older than she, and at college, she did not meet anyone she thought was their equal.

Bob and Betty finally met in late summer of 1932, when they both attended a tennis party in Oak Park hosted by Chick Heile, who was the best friend of Betty's brother Stewart, and also a friend of Bob's from Oak Park High School. Bob found Betty very attractive, and was impressed by the spunky way she defended herself from the advances of their married host while playing "sardines," a game where everyone tried to stuff themselves into the same closet.[19] After the party, they all trooped down to Bob's apartment in Chicago to listen to his jazz records. There she further wowed him by knowing all the words to the songs on his records. However, she was initially much more attracted to his roommate, Jim Snydacker, a fraternity mate of his from Cornell, and was not particularly interested in Bob.

Both men visited her in Milwaukee after the first meeting, but Jim yielded to Bob's insistence that he had seen her first, and she then did fall in love with Bob.[20] She appreciated his attentiveness and admired his culture and education. Indeed, she had finally found someone similar to her brothers and father.

Bob exploited the Frank Lloyd Wright connection, taking her to Taliesin twice in the early stages of their courtship. Her November 2 letter after the

---

[18] Unpublished letters to his children, "The Girls of Oak Park" and "Ten Cents a Dance."

[19] The information in these two paragraphs about their first meeting comes from the 1989 videotaped interviews with Betty.

[20] Betty's initial interest in Jim can be glimpsed in Letter No. 1, where she coyly says, "I like Jim very much and was glad he was with us" and encourages the two of them to drive up to visit her. Bob's reaction to that in Letter No. 2, and her growing interest in Bob in the subsequent letters, demonstrate how he did succeed in winning her heart.

Halloween party there shows that her interest in him is clearly growing. Betty's recounting of these first visits to Taliesin in her taped memoirs shows that she was titillated at the prospect of visiting what she imagined to be a "den of iniquity" from the press reports at that time. She did find the other guests very interesting, and thought Olgivanna, Wright's third wife, was quite glamorous, but found the atmosphere at Taliesin then and later quite "puritanical," contrary to her expectations. She also discovered on the second visit that Frank Lloyd Wright had known her father. The letters show that by mid-December she is planning to use her Christmas vacation time for two four- to five-day visits with Bob in Chicago, and is reading Frank Lloyd Wright's recently published *Autobiography,* which for her is a book about Bob. He declares his love for her in writing on December 14, and she reciprocates on January 3, when they both start talking about finding her a job in Chicago and their marriage plans.

The biggest stumbling block to marriage was their financial situation. Bob wanted to amass more money before they embarked on marriage and, though he was in favor of her working, he also wanted to be able to support both of them. He was just starting a private law practice, however, and in this period of economic depression was having difficulty making it pay. While Betty had a job, she was often not paid for months at a time due to the State of Wisconsin's financial problems.

Their geographical separation was another obstacle they faced. Milwaukee and Chicago are about ninety miles apart, and their living and working in separate cities did not allow them to date in the usual sense. Instead they had to take trips to see each other, and the letters show that this was a financial as well as emotional hardship on them.[21]

They both wanted to find employment for her in Chicago in order to ease this strain on their emotions and pocketbooks. However, it was extremely

---

[21] The letters provide a fair amount of information about this aspect of their situation. Betty apparently worked a full day Monday through Friday plus Saturday mornings, which meant they could only see each other on weekends, often for just a day and a half; their only lengthier stays were during vacations. They rode back and forth for these trips on the North Shore electric train, which at the time had frequent trips between the two cities. Neither of them owned cars, though Bob occasionally borrowed one, and Betty occasionally got a ride from friends. The fare was $3 round-trip, with occasional $1 excursions. Betty did not pay for her lodging when she traveled to Chicago, as she stayed with Bob's or her brother Stewart's friends, while Bob paid $1 a night for rooms Betty found him in Milwaukee. In her videotaped memoirs, Betty recounted that during the early period of Bob's courtship of her, her brother Stewart invited her to Chicago and sent her a ticket. She eventually learned that Bob had paid for the ticket and "set the whole thing up." This was probably the weekend of November 12–13, which she refers to in Letter No.6.

difficult for her to find another job during the economic depression, and despite great efforts on both their parts, continuing until right before their marriage and afterwards, they never succeeded in this endeavor.

Betty was more optimistic than Bob about their financial prospects. She believed he would succeed as a lawyer despite his current financial difficulties.[22] She also felt that she would be able to contribute some money to the marriage, despite anxiety over the irregular payments of her salary, due to the economic difficulties faced by the State of Wisconsin during this period.[23] Even though Bob failed to amass the money he thought was necessary for their marriage, she went ahead and took the risk of giving up her job in Milwaukee to join him in Chicago.

For Betty, Bob's love gave her an emotional security she had never felt before,[24] and financial security was not as important. She had been less spoiled than Bob in this regard, as once her stepfather embarked on his career as a minister her family was not wealthy. After her father died when she was still a teenager, only her older brother Gordon gave her some extra financial support,

---

[22] "Someone passed a clipping around the office yesterday which made me feel very optimistic. It related the finds of a survey on the incomes in professional and skilled occupations. Doctors and lawyers were highest, the lawyers earning an average of over $5000 a year. Think what we'll do with that in a few years' time. Nothing could make me believe that you're not way above average in legal ability so that should mean much more for us. I'm on the point of deciding what colleges our six children should go to—anyway, aside from such foolishness, I think you're a smart guy, and I'm even willing to admit that a doctor's degree surpasses a Phi Beta Kappa key (Letter No. 37)." While in later years, Bob did in fact earn $5,000 and more (see below in this Introduction), at the time he reported earning only $120 for the month of February 1933 (Letter No. 44) and recounted several tales of woe about not getting paid: once because his client had all her money in one of the few banks that failed to reopen (Letter No. 65), a second time due to a settlement he turned down because he wanted more money in order to marry Betty (Letter No. 80), and a third from losing a preliminary injunction in court (Letter No. 107). Though he wanted to "start married life with five or six hundred dollars in the bank" (ibid.) he in fact had only amassed, to his deep shame, $25 in personal cash resources three weeks before their marriage on July 29, 1933 (Letter No. 137).

[23] In her taped memoirs, Betty recalled that her job paid $1,100 a year, and that the rent for her "great room" overlooking Lake Michigan was very affordable at that salary. This figure is slightly less than the $99 a month median wage for women clerical workers in 1931 reported by William H. Chafe, in a passage about the "inadequate pay" for women workers in every job category [*The Paradox of Change, American Women in the 20th Century* (New York & Oxford: Oxford UP, 1991), 74]. She apparently was not getting any money from her parents, either, as she was shocked when her mother sent her $50 as a wedding gift. She didn't know whether to keep it or not, as she had never known her mother and stepfather to have that much money at once (Letter No. 152).

[24] "When he proposed, I burst into tears. I was so emotionally deprived in my childhood, and it just overwhelmed me that somebody loved me enough to want to live with me." (Betty's videotaped memoirs).

which was not automatic.[25] She was thus used to living with less money than Bob was, as he had freely accepted the generosity of both of his parents, who rarely denied him anything.[26] At the time he met Betty, however, he was trying to establish his financial independence. He wanted to be able to support the two of them on his own money, and avoid his father's pattern of indebtedness. Because his current earnings were not very substantial, he also was taking a risk by agreeing to a marriage where he would be the sole support for the couple.

They were married in a simple church ceremony on July 29, 1933, with only a few local friends and family in attendance. Bob's brother Dave had to provide food for the wedding party at the last minute, as the bride and groom had neglected to think about this, and they spent their honeymoon in a local hotel using Betty's brother Stewart's "due bills."[27] They only began living together in Bob's basement apartment in Chicago two weeks later, as she had to work the first two weeks of August in order to earn her vacation time and be paid through September 1.[28]

Betty's optimism about Bob's earning power proved to be well founded.[29] She was still unable to find anything other than volunteer work in Chicago, but he always provided for her and the family they soon created together. His private practice may never have been as successful as he hoped, and they initially lived on a strict budget of $95 a month, but it was enough to get by. When Betty became pregnant with their first child, Thomas Llewellyn, born July 26, 1935, Bob went to work for Montgomery Ward, where he earned $5,000 a year.

---

25 Betty's videotaped memoirs, and a letter to her from her brother Gordon dated November 23, 1930, found filed with the courtship letters.

26 Unpublished letters to his children, "Your Father's Recollections of His Father" and "Not Making It in the Twenties."

27 Betty's videotaped memoirs. A "due bill" is a written acknowledgment of indebtedness, but I have not been able to find any information about how such an instrument might have been used to pay for lodging in a hotel.

28 Letters No. 114 and 168.

29 The following paragraphs are drawn from my own family memories and Betty's videotaped memoirs.

12. Betty pregnant, taken by a street photographer in Oak Park

13. Betty with her son Tom

Shortly after the birth of Timothy Kehler, their second child, on May 6, 1938, Bob went to work for the Justice Department in Washington, DC. His salary at that time was $6,000 a year, and Betty remembered that they lived better in those first years in Washington than ever before or since. Their third and last child, Elizabeth Catherine, was born on September 8, 1943. After a number of years as an attorney in the Antitrust Division of the Justice Department, Bob moved again into private practice. He then went into government work once more, as chief counsel for the Patent Subcommittee of the U.S. Senate Judiciary Committee. Later, Lee Loevinger, who had been appointed by President Kennedy to head the Antitrust Division, invited Bob to join him as first assistant. After Loevinger was appointed to another government position, Bob was gradually eased out. He finished his career in private practice again, until his heart condition prevented him from continuing to try cases.

The family lived comfortably in suburban Maryland during the years Bob worked in Washington, DC. When Elizabeth was around eleven, Betty found paid work again, not so much out of financial necessity as from her own desire to do so. She began working part-time in the Washington DC Public Library, and then earned her MA in library science from Catholic University in 1956, the same year her second son graduated from high school. The couple was even able to realize their dream of building a Frank Lloyd Wright house, though they had to reduce the size and scope of the original plan to one that cost $40,000 rather than $80,000. They moved into it in the fall of 1957, when Elizabeth was fourteen. Betty continued working in the DC public library system until her retirement in 1974.

14. Betty, 1958, reading in the living room of the Frank Lloyd Wright house she and Bob built, with photo of Frank Lloyd Wright on shelf

The emotional component of their marriage was less stable than the financial situation. During the courtship period, Betty had enjoyed Bob's complete attentiveness to her when they saw each other on weekends. Once their married life began in Chicago, however, this changed to a routine where he played tennis with other friends for most of every weekend. He even went to movies by himself during the week when he didn't have much work, without calling her to join him. This was a great disappointment and disillusionment to Betty, who expected to continue the close companionship she had experienced with him while they were courting. He did find her a volunteer job in Chicago at the League of Nations library, which she enjoyed, and her pregnancies always brought her a period of contentment. However, the actual raising of children was much more difficult for her, and she continued to want more time with her husband alone. Instead, he began spending even longer periods away from her and the children through the travel necessitated by his job with the Justice Department. When she complained, he replied that he enjoyed traveling and did not want to give up that part of his job.

Even as she struggled with Bob's lack of attentiveness to her emotional needs, Betty still held Bob in great esteem and never wanted to leave him. She sought help to deal with her emotional insecurity and unhappiness, and spoke out about her complaints, rather than retreating into illness as her mother had. Her continued admiration for him, and focus on him rather than on the children, fed his ego enough that he did not feel the temptation to leave that his father had experienced, and instead remained a constant husband and father.

Thus while the great love they expressed in the letters no longer manifested itself so overtly during their marriage, the security they provided for each other did allow them to break from the pattern set by their parents, and give their children a more stable family life than they had experienced. Their shared trauma as youngest children abandoned by their fathers certainly helped to form a profound connection between them, and they remained together through over fifty years of marriage.

Betty devoted herself to Bob's care without complaint during the last two years of his life, until he died of congestive heart failure on February 22, 1986, at the age of eighty-two. She flourished for several years after his death, taking up weaving, traveling to many different countries, and engaging in volunteer work for women's organizations and the Textile Museum library. She began to suffer from ministrokes in 1995, after a heart operation, and moved into a retirement community in 1996. She then entered full nursing care in early 1997 after a fall accelerated her downward spiral into senile dementia. It was clear, however, that she was still experiencing a rich inner life even as she became less and less communicative with her children and the outside world. She died on November 17, 2005, at the age of ninety-five.

15. Betty in the 1980s – widow and world traveler

Betty displayed contradictory characteristics of assertiveness and deference in her behavior with Bob, both in their courtship correspondence and throughout their lives together. She was well educated and capable of financial and intellectual independence, and often had a rebellious spirit. However, her difficult childhood had left Betty emotionally insecure and lacking in self-esteem. She wanted very much to get married, and equated that with success for a woman. Finding love from a man she admired helped her believe more in her own worth, despite all the difficulties she experienced with Bob later. As she said in her taped memoirs: "I couldn't bring myself to reread our correspondence until after he died, and then it was a tremendous comfort to me to feel that I had been loved so much."

Bob also experienced emotional trauma during his childhood and adolescent years due to his father's departure from the family. Although his mother's devotion and his father's financial generosity gave him more security than Betty experienced during her adolescence, he became quite emotionally closed. His brothers and sisters were all quite outspoken in their defense of either their mother or father, and he repeated often that he had not wanted to "choose sides" as they had. This strategy undoubtedly stabilized him at the time, but the whole experience left him rather emotionally and sexually repressed. While he was quite gregarious, he had difficulty forming satisfactory relationships with women before he met Betty.

The bond of love they formed with each other thus allowed both of them to reach a degree of contentment and self-confidence they had not previously known. Their courtship letters, where they struggle to express their feelings for each other, are sassy and witty but also poignant, as during the correspondence the two of them gradually develop the courage to love and be loved, and commit to a lasting relationship.

Complete Annotated Letters

Part One: Falling In Love

Letters 1–15, October 15, 1932–January 3, 1933

1. Milwaukee, Saturday [October 15, 1932][30]

Dear Bob –

I have tried to write you several times this week and have failed not for lack of inspiration but for the reason that I was trying to play bridge or talk to people or listen to football games at the same time. Now I'm really putting my mind on it.

I really can't tell you how much I enjoyed the weekend because it can't have been so new and interesting and exciting to you[31] as it was to me. I can't ever remember having as satisfying a visit. I like Jim[32] very much and was glad he was with us –

I have felt very much in the mood for a trip to Chicago lately, what with your excellent sales talk and a general restlessness I feel now that you have stirred me from my little rut but I cannot. I mean I really can't, I must have just gone crazy last month because I haven't a cent and I shall spend a quiet October in Milwaukee. I'm sure that I can and shall come either the first or second weekend in November, however.

In the meantime, I should like it very much if you and Jim could drive up here. Will you please consider it seriously?

Sincerely, Betty

---

30 For clarity, I have added the city from which each letter is sent, from information on the envelopes or on the letterhead. I put the day or the date in brackets when it is not supplied in the letter, to show that Betty often puts only the day of the week and not the date, and that Bob often puts only the date but not the day of the week, something he mentions in Letter No.86.

31 The phrase "to you" is added above the line. In this transcription of the letters I have added all such inserts to the main text, for greater ease of reading (see Illustration 16b).

32 Jim Snydacker, Bob's apartment mate at the time. Betty was initially quite interested in him, and not particularly attracted to Bob (see "Introduction" above).

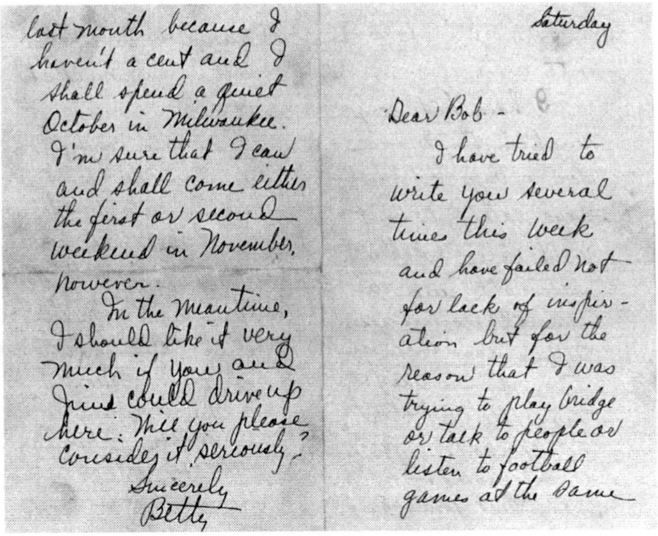

last month because I
haven't a cent and I
shall spend a quiet
October in Milwaukee.
I'm sure that I can
and shall come either
the first or second
weekend in November,
however.
In the meantime,
I should like it very
much if you and
Jim could drive up
here. Will you please
consider it seriously?
Sincerely
Betty

Saturday

Dear Bob -
I have tried to
write you several
times this week
and have failed not
for lack of inspir-
ation but for the
reason that I was
trying to play bridge
or talk to people or
listen to football
games at the same

16a. Letter No. 1, first and last pages

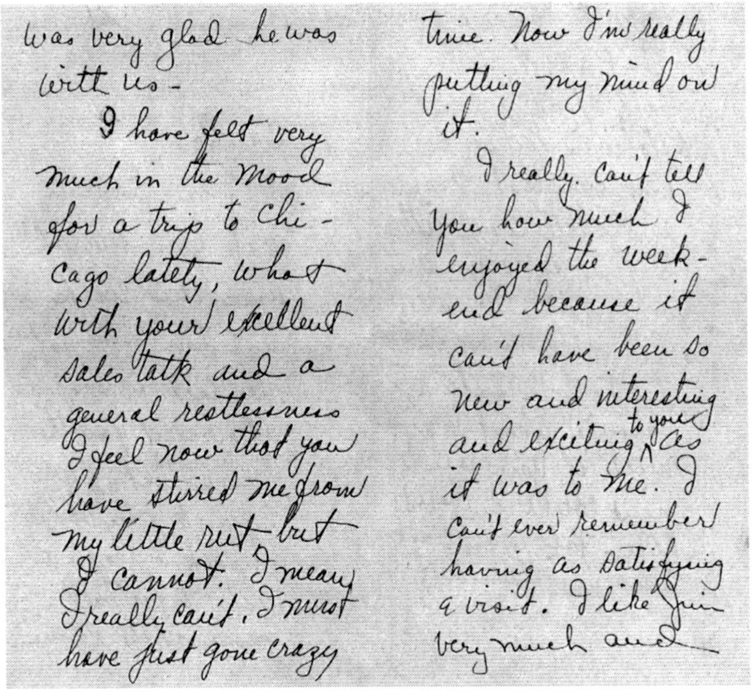

was very glad he was
with us -
I have felt very
much in the mood
for a trip to Chi-
cago lately, what
with your excellent
sales talk and a
general restlessness
I feel now that you
have stirred me from
my little rut but
I cannot. I mean
I really can't. I must
have just gone crazy

time. Now I'm really
putting my mind on
it.
I really can't tell
you how much I
enjoyed the week-
end because it
can't have been so
new and interesting
and exciting to you as
it was to me. I
can't ever remember
having as satisfying
a visit. I like Jim
very much and

16b. Letter No. 1, second and third pages

2. Chicago, [Wednesday] Oct. 19, 1932

Dear Betty,

I was awfully glad to get your letter and happy to know that you enjoyed our trip. I might add that Jim was quite flattered to hear what you said about him as he also likes you very much and if he doesn't succeed in occupying a considerable amount of your time and attention I shall be greatly surprised. However, when you added that you were "very glad he was with us" I felt constrained to repeat the words made immortal by that superb sardine player, Chick Heile, "What's the matter–don't you trust me?" [33]

Your decision not to come to Chicago until November was disappointing and it looks as though we shall have a difficult time seeing each other while we are both broke. The solution lies in one of us becoming richer and inasmuch as I would prefer to become richer anyway, I will[34] undertake the responsibility of becoming richer for both of us.

In the meantime I should like to lay before you a temporary solution. You made an ultra-favorable impression upon my step-mother and she has directed me to ask you to attend the annual Halloween party at Taliesin, which occurs on the 29th of this month.[35] I have never been to one of these parties myself and I am afraid that, due to the presence of numerous out of town guests, the overnight accommodations[36] may be somewhat crowded but I would like very much to take a chance on liking it if you will. I also want to show you some of the surrounding country that the rain kept us from seeing last time. If you can

---

[33] Chick Heile was the host of the party where Bob and Betty first met (See "Introduction" above).

[34] The word "will" is written over the word "shall" in the handwritten letter. In this transcription, I have added all such overwrites to the main text and deleted cross-outs, for greater ease of reading (see Illustration 17b).

[35] Bob's stepmother was Olgivanna, Frank Lloyd Wright's third wife, and Taliesin is the residence Wright built on his mother's family land in Wisconsin, begun initially in 1911 as a home where he could live with his lover Mamah Borthwick Cheney. By the date of this letter, it had caught on fire and been rebuilt three times, and Wright was entering a period of relative stability following his marriage to Olgivanna and the formal opening of the Taliesin Fellowship in October of 1932. I have not been able to find any documentation other than these letters concerning the Halloween party of 1932.

[36] The word is spelled "accomodations" in the text. In this transcription of the letters, I have corrected a few accidental spelling errors such as this one, but have otherwise maintained the original spelling, grammar, and punctuation found in the letters.

go with me I will borrow a car from my mother or brother, drive to Milwaukee on Saturday morning, drive you out Saturday afternoon and back Sunday night.

I am afraid I have committed a tactical error in letting you know that I want so much to see you, but let me hear from you as soon as possible.

Bob

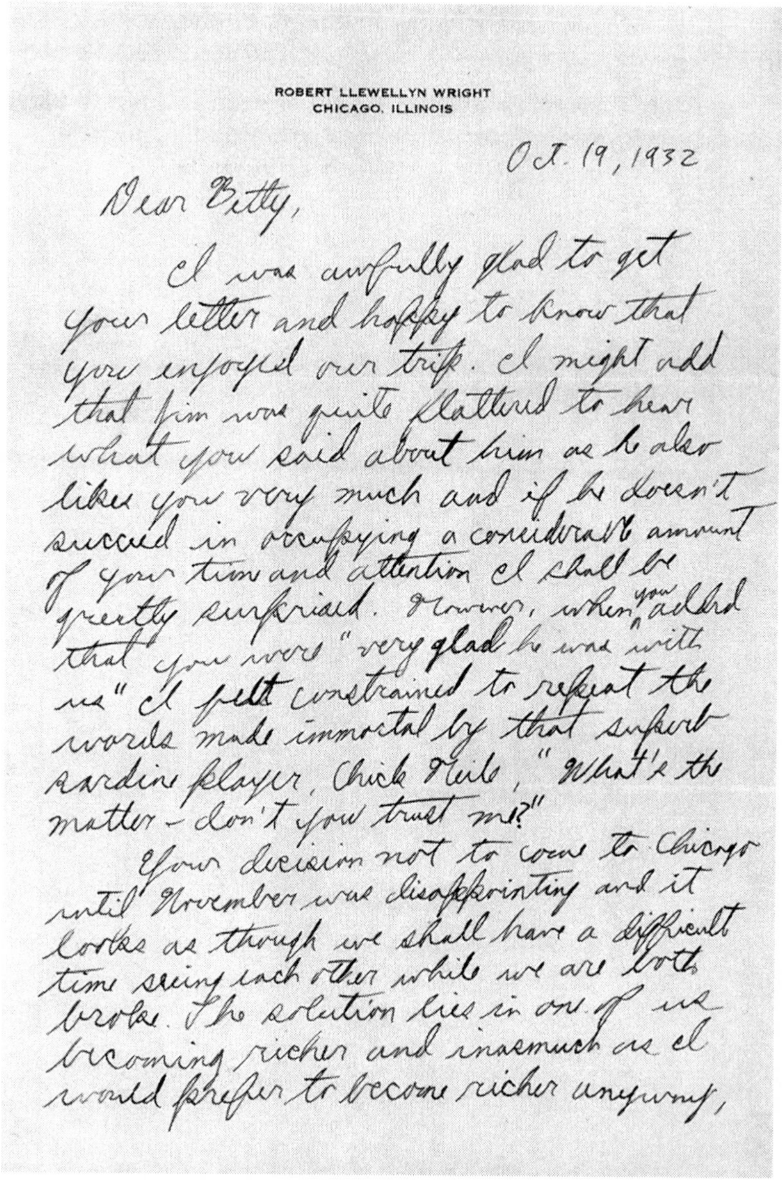

ROBERT LLEWELLYN WRIGHT
CHICAGO, ILLINOIS

Oct. 19, 1932

Dear Betty,

I was awfully glad to get your letter and happy to know that you enjoyed our trip. I might add that Jim was quite flattered to hear what you said about him as he also likes you very much and if he doesn't succeed in occupying a considerable amount of your time and attention I shall be greatly surprised. However, when you added that you were "very glad he was with us" I felt constrained to repeat the words made immortal by that superb sardine player, Chick Neils, "What's the matter – don't you trust me?"

Your decision not to come to Chicago until November was disappointing and it looks as though we shall have a difficult time seeing each other while we are both broke. The solution lies in one of us becoming richer and inasmuch as I would prefer to become richer anyway,

17a. Letter No.2, recto

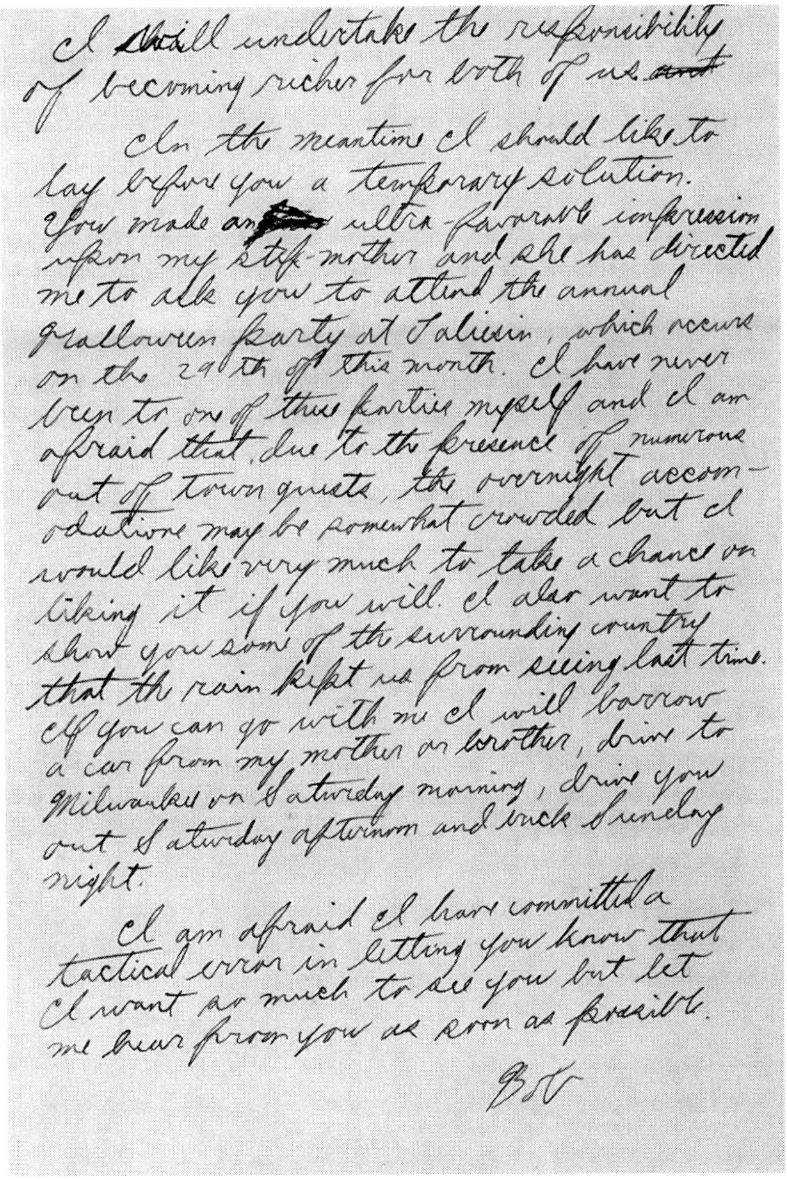

I ~~shall~~ will undertake the responsibility
of becoming richer for both of us. ~~and~~

In the meantime I should like to
lay before you a temporary solution.
You made an ~~[illegible]~~ ultra-favorable impression
upon my step-mother and she has directed
me to ask you to attend the annual
Halloween party at Taliesin, which occurs
on the 29th of this month. I have never
been to one of these parties myself and I am
afraid that, due to the presence of numerous
out of town guests, the overnight accomodations may be somewhat crowded but I
would like very much to take a chance on
liking it if you will. I also want to
show you some of the surrounding country
that the rain kept us from seeing last time.
If you can go with me I will borrow
a car from my mother or brother, drive to
Milwaukee on Saturday morning, drive you
out Saturday afternoon and back Sunday
night.

I am afraid I have committed a
tactical error in letting you know that
I want so much to see you but let
me hear from you as soon as possible.

Bob

17b. Letter No. 2, verso

3. Milwaukee, Monday [October 24, 1932]

Dear Bob,

I'd love to go to the Hallowe'en party. I know I'll like it and I insist upon your liking it also -

I rode horseback [fo]r[37] two hours yester[da]y with practic[ally] no ill effects—no asthma, I mean. I am rather stiff- I'm telling you about it because I thought you might possibly want to ride next week and if it's cold enough I'm sure I can -

Your letter li[fted] a great bur[den] from my m[ind]. Someone is always mentioning that Heile incident and never, until I read your quotation, have I been able to remember anything about it. It all comes back to me now - [It?] must have been [very?] funny -

I shall be home anytime after twelve-thirty on Saturday, and shall be expecting you.

Sincerely, Betty

4. Milwaukee, Tuesday [November 1, 1932]

Dear Bob -

I am writing you with a certain intensity of purpose because if I don't do it now I know I won't for some time. We're going through a period of hysteria known as junior transfer week.[38] I have Thursday off but it doesn't mean much because I have to stay in town for a meeting at night.

Yesterday Edris[39] walked into the office. She is opening up Milwaukee for Hexri this week, and apparently doing a swell job of it. Mr. Savery also walked in, quite independently of her, and we all had dinner together. It was

---

37 This letter is torn, so I have filled in with brackets what I assume are the missing letters.

38 Betty worked at the Milwaukee Vocational School, as the receptionist for a group of counselors (see "Introduction" above).

39 In her videotaped memoirs, Betty mentions Edris as a woman doctor, who gave her advice about birth control, and was a friend of Elinor (Nell), whom her brother Stewart later married. In subsequent letters, Betty mentions Edris as someone with whom she can stay while visiting Bob in Chicago, and she also borrows money from her at one point.

very pleasant but I'm still a little weary from the weekend. (I hope I don't have to tell you that I consider it well worth its cost in fatigue.)

I've been doing research for you in my spare time. I can't find our friend the drunk in either directory. If 332 N. 14 St is not the correct address, will you send it to me and I'll look again? The switchboard operator called Western Union about the telegrams. It may surprise you to know that they were sent just to Milwaukee—no other address. Western Union seemed just a bit amused about it all. The Thompson waitresses must be more distracting than I would imagine.

I can't explain to you why I have not decided when I shall come to Chicago because I have just one sheet of stationery. I have good and sufficient reasons and in due time I shall come and I'll let you know, of course.

I had an exceptionally good time over the weekend. You have made an impression on me now, and I'm full of theories about you - none very lucid, I admit. I think you're pretty nice to me and I don't know just why, for all our conversation. Please don't destroy all my egotism, will you?

Betty

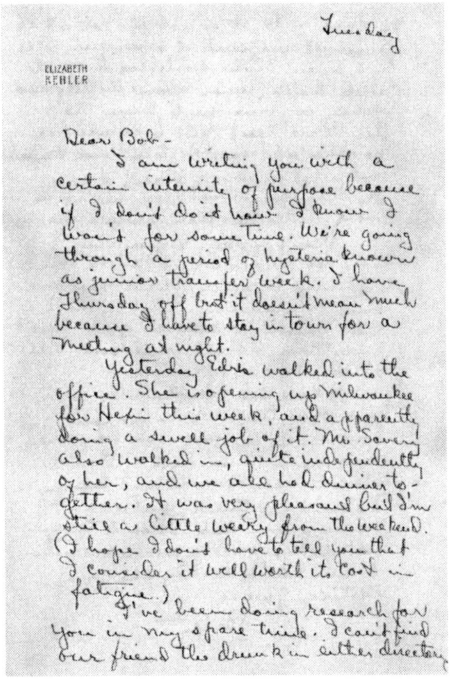
Tuesday

ELIZABETH
KEHLER

Dear Bob -
I am writing you with a certain intensity of purpose because if I don't do it now I know I won't for some time. We're going through a period of hysteria known as junior transfer week. I have Thursday off but it doesn't mean much because I have to stay in town for a meeting at night.
Yesterday Edris walked into the office. She is opening up Milwaukee for Hepi this week, and apparently doing a swell job of it. Mr. Savery also walked in, quite independently of her, and we all had dinner together. It was very pleasant but I'm still a little weary from the weekend. (I hope I don't have to tell you that I consider it well worth its cost in fatigue.)
I've been doing research for you in my spare time. I can't find our friend the drunk in either directory

18. Letter No. 4, recto, Elizabeth Kehler letterhead

5. Chicago, [Sunday] Nov. 6, 1932

Dear Betty,

Your letter was both encouraging and disappointing. I was gratified to learn that you have theories about me but put out by your indifference toward the research work necessary to supply you with the facts, by which to test them. Of your many indecisions, the one concerning your next visit to Chicago is to me the most painful and if you persist in staying away it will be regarded as a personal affront.

Stewart and Nell dropped in today, Stewart reporting that you wrote him you wanted to come down soon.[40] You might at least see that your stories check.

Thank you very much for trying to locate my automobile antagonist but inasmuch as the bill for the fender was only two dollars I feel inclined to let the whole matter drop. The size of the bill has increased my embarrassment over the scene created and I hereby apologize to you again for it. Your behaviour under the annoying circumstances scored you another 100 in deportment and brought your average in that department to a very high point.

I had had some theories about you, right from the start, and was just getting ready to set down on paper for you the one that I thought most logical, but only to find that my theories have changed to feelings, which are difficult for me to express at any time and almost impossible to write about. This is alarming and something may have to be done about it. At least my thoughts will have to be cleared of their excessive preoccupation with you if I am to continue to carry out the routine of a law practice, with safety to myself and clients.

My greatest fear is that you will decide to come to Chicago on Thanksgiving, when I probably won't be here. Why don't you come this week-end and resolve all doubts.

Bob

---

40 Stewart was the younger of Betty's two brothers, eight years older than she, and one year older than Bob. He lived in Chicago at the time of the letters, and had taken her to the party at Chick Heile's where they met. Stewart, Bob, and Chick had all attended Oak Park High School together before Bob transferred out to the Francis W. Parker School in his junior year. Nell was at this time separated from her first husband, and after she obtained a divorce, she and Stewart married, in late June or early July of 1933, shortly before Betty and Bob. See Letters No. 123 and 127.

6. Milwaukee, [Thursday November 17 1932]

Dear Bob-

The opening of a letter is always hard for me. Everything I want to say seems too abrupt for an opening. Now that I have evaded it in this way I can say what I have on my mind.

There were several statements I wanted to make to you before I left but I was too dazed both Sunday night and Monday morning to bring them forth. One is that I have never had anyone display toward me the considerate attention which you did last weekend.[41] You may have thought that I missed some of the finer points of your conduct but I assure you that I did not.

Another thing that impressed me was the amazing way in which you improve upon acquaintance. I am torn between two courses as a result: whether to utilize every opportunity to see if it can possibly go on like this, or to run like hell in the other direction. If you still need a clue to my character, there's a major one.

I hardly need state after this almost complete breakdown of reserve on my part that I enjoyed the weekend. May I cite for particular merit, however, the first half of Saturday evening and all of Sunday with the exception of the Newberry Theatre[42] disaster? On the other hand don't ever try to build up that seven-five train to me again. I know that I was entirely responsible but I am now convinced that eleven-thirty five is an awfully nice hour.[43]

I felt swell on Monday but I displayed positive imagination in making mistakes in the office which just can't be remedied. Fortunately, I am the only one who knows of them so far. After twenty-four hours of sleep in the last two nights I feel almost normal.

---

41 In her videotaped memoirs, Betty mentioned that she later learned that Bob, unbeknownst to her, gave Stewart money to pay for her fare to Chicago for this first visit after they went to the Taliesin party together. See n. 21.

42 "The Newberry [cinema] opened in 1914 and had seating for 700. The theater was located on Clark Street at Chestnut Street. It was named for its location not far from the famed Newberry Library. The Newberry became a porn theater in the early 1970s (first straight for a short time, then gay) until the theater closed around 1977. It was afterward torn down and replaced by a parking lot, which is still there today" (http://cinematreasures.org/theater/8380/).

43 Betty and Bob went back and forth from Milwaukee to Chicago on the North Shore electric train, which had frequent trips between the two cities at the time.

I am very grateful to Linda for teaching me that song. I shall be singing happily to myself for a month now. It's almost the only recreation I need anyway.

Tell your roommate that he may call me Bessie if he wishes –

Sincerely, Betty

[written sideways in left margin]: P.S. I am sacrificing my pride by writing to you on this stationery so you'd better like it.[44] (There's something a little odd about my grammar there, but I don't know what it is.) My mother always annoys me by writing around the edges like this. I now discover there's a strange fascination about it. I can hardly stop, I like it so much –

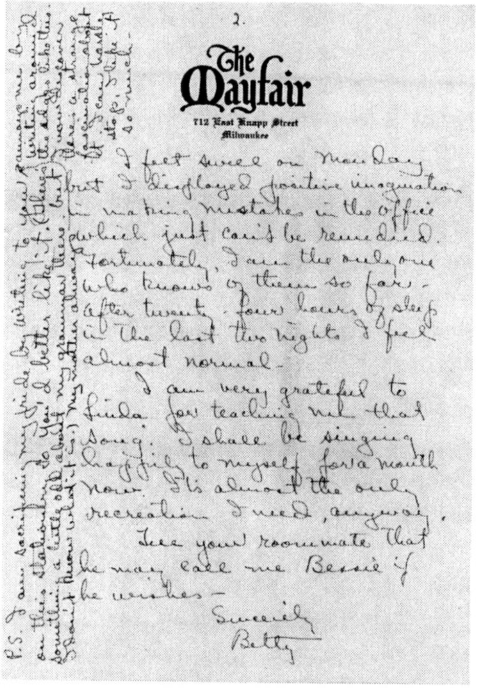
2.

The Mayfair
712 East Knapp Street
Milwaukee

I felt swell on Monday but I displayed positive imagination in making mistakes in the office which just can't be remedied. Fortunately, I am the only one who knows of them so far. After twenty-four hours of sleep in the last two nights I feel almost normal.

I am very grateful to Linda for teaching me that song. I shall be singing happily to myself for a month now. It's almost the only recreation I need, anyway.

Tell your roommate that he may call me Bessie if he wishes –

Sincerely,
Betty

P.S. I am sacrificing my pride by writing to you on this stationery so you'd better like it. (There's something a little odd about my grammar there, but I don't know what it is.) My mother always annoys me by writing around the edges like this. I now discover there's a strange fascination about it. I can hardly stop, I like it so much –

19. Letter No. 6, last page, with Mayfair letterhead and writing up the side of the page

44 The stationery has the letterhead "The Mayfair, 712 East Knapp Street, Milwaukee" (see Illustration No. 19). The building is still extant in Milwaukee, and is now a rooming house. According to the man who was the manager of the building in October 2005, it was built in 1926, and was previously a hotel until around the year 2000.

7. Chicago, [Thursday] Dec. 1, 1932 [sent Special Delivery]

Dear Betty,

Ever since I talked to you on the phone Tuesday I had been walking on air until your letter[45] brought me to earth with a crash, this evening. You see, when you told me that you might visit me Sunday I felt for the first time that perhaps you wanted to see me as badly as I wanted to see you, in spite of the indifference indicated by your failure to write, because I knew that riding down here and back on the train in one day meant a considerable effort for you, or anyone. But now you assure me that I am all wrong "about everything."

You then tell me that you may come to Chicago this week-end but that you "don't approve" of the trip, which will apparently be made, if at all, against your will. This is all too much for me to understand but without any understanding I know still that I want to see you and talk to you and be with you any where I can at any time I can, more than I want anything else.

Please come Sunday if you can't come Saturday and if you can come Saturday I can assure you that Nell will be delighted to have you spend the night with her. If I don't get a wire from you tomorrow morning about Saturday don't fail to let me know about Sunday.

There are a great many things that I want to say to you but in the present state of our correspondence I hardly dare mention them. I want to talk to you soon because I'm sure that you can't talk as ambiguously as you write.

Bob

8. Milwaukee, Monday [December 5, 1932]

Dear Bob -

Mr. Patterson gave me next Saturday morning off with no hesitation so you may expect me at six o'clock or some such time on Friday evening. Assuming that there is a four o'clock train and that I catch it, I think it should arrive at Grand Avenue at five-fifty-three. I shall write Stewart and he can probably meet me unless you particularly want to.

---

[45] This letter appears to be missing.

I am glad that you haven't my conservative and practical turn of mind for if you had you wouldn't have come yesterday. It was a pretty impressive performance and I liked it.

I am closing now because I feel that letters are my least satisfactory method of expressing myself.

I am saving my next swoon for you. I hope you liked it.

Betty

9. Milwaukee, Monday [December 12, 1932]

Dear Bob-

My optimism was too great, and I became the goat of the employment department this morning and was assigned next week as my vacation. I don't quite know what to do about it. I was offered an alternative of a long weekend around Christmas and another around New Year's but couldn't seem to get it through my dull skull and chose the simpler arrangement.

I have, of course, planned to spend my week with you. Nell's being away complicates matters. I don't like the thought of being there all alone and I don't imagine Edris will be at home either. I plan to write Stewart tomorrow to see what he thinks about it.

Besides that I had counted on at least two weeks without you to try to do some clear thinking. I am terrifically upset about you and me and terribly afraid of what I may do to you. It seems to me that my reactions toward being without you for a while are of great importance right now.

I know that I should never try to put down on paper anything so confused as my emotions are right now. Please don't try too hard to understand this because you may misinterpret it entirely. I certainly don't intend to upset you. Just trying to write about it has, however, helped me to feel less tragic about it all. Am I being perfectly clear?

Do you mind my being just a little nuts? I've just had a complete change of mind in one paragraph. Everything seems swell and I'm not worried in the least about past, present or future. I should begin the letter all over again but it's much too late for that. All this should convince you of one thing. You have me in a state.

All the things I meant to say to you about what a swell time I had, what I think about your Christmas present and how I could worry about that if I put my mind on it which I refuse to do and how much I like the Bissells—all these you will have to imagine right now.

Please laugh at me, Bob, because I'm laughing at myself.

Betty

10. Milwaukee, Tuesday [December 13, 1932]

Dear Bob,

If you would throw away unread nine out of every ten letters I write you both of us would be better off. Even the factual information which I tried to give you is wrong because I have changed my mind about my vacation.

This is my present plan. (I won't dare change my mind again so you can rely on this.) My vacation will start Thursday the 22nd. I can come to Chicago Wednesday night and stay until Saturday or Sunday when I hope Stewart will take me to Madison.[46] If he doesn't I'll go anyway. I will stay there until Tuesday, go to Milwaukee and work Wednesday and Thursday and return to Chicago Thursday night (the 29th) and stay Friday, Saturday, Sunday and Monday.

If you have a calendar in front of you as I have this really becomes somewhat simpler. Perhaps, being my intellectual superior, you don't find it as difficult as I do.

This arrangement really seems better to me and I trust that it will be more convenient for you. I don't want to disturb your plans for Christmas, of course. Whether I am in town or not, please go to Gary[47] when you have planned and when you are expected. I must still submit this plan to Stewart and after he has told me what he thinks and you have told me what you think about it perhaps I'll make a definite statement.

I feel so sane today that I don't understand how I could write you that silly letter last night.

Please write me very soon, won't you? I'm terribly anxious to see you and even a letter will help a little.

Betty

---

46 Betty and Stewart's mother and stepfather were living in Madison, Wisconsin at the time of the courtship.

47 Bob's mother was living in Gary, Indiana, at the time of the courtship, possibly with Ben Page, whom she had married in 1930. See n. 6.

11. Chicago, [Wednesday, December 14, 1932]

Dear Betty,

Will you please autograph and return the enclosed photograph to me? By covering the eye and ear you will see that in this pose Miss Garbo looks more like you than you do yourself. I am serious about your returning it because I haven't any picture of you and this will have to do until I get one.[48] This brings me to the next enclosure, the article on "Love Letters", which I fortunately ran across before writing this or I probably would have turned so cute on you as to open it with "Dear Greta." After reading the article you will understand why I write you with fear and trembling.[49] We both know that the language of love letters is so stilted and sentimental that the effect is often sickening yet I don't see how I can honestly write you anything but a love letter. I'll make it simple - I love you.

Having just written what no lawyer in his right mind would ever put on paper I find the definitely insane state of mind evidenced by your letter of Monday, which reached me tonight along with your calm letter of Tuesday, encouraging rather than disappointing, although I'll confess that when I left you Sunday night I felt that I had rather let you down at the finish of our week-end and that you were disgusted with me. Of course, I haven't told you anything that you weren't already aware of if feminine intuition is all that they say it is but knowing how you feel about security in general I thought your emotional security might be strengthened if you had it down in black and white; perhaps even filed away for ready reference should a doubt arise. When I say "it" I mean "I love you."

With this off my chest, or rather heart, I feel able to write to you more calmly and intelligently about your vacation plans. Your second idea of two week-ends instead of a week seems much better for you and is ideal as far as I

---

48 No photograph was found in the envelope.

49 The original enclosure was present in the envelope, and is in fact a story clipped from *The New Yorker* entitled "Love Letters," by Sally Benson. The principal characters are Elizabeth Montgomery and Bob McEwen, and Elizabeth recounts her disgust and disappointment with most of the letters she received from men she dated: "She wondered why so many kind, intelligent men went wrong the minute they got hold of a pen and a piece of paper. They wrote things they would never dream of saying. Men who were comfortably inarticulate when they were face to face with her went practically elfin on paper. They tried to show her that there was more to them than she had thought. They tried to surprise her. And they did." Waiting for a letter from Bob, she is braced for the worst, and happily relieved when she gets a simple note saying he wants to see her again (*The New Yorker*, December 10, 1932, 20–21).

am concerned but I don't understand why you hesitate to stay at Nell's alone. You will be perfectly safe there and are certainly self-sufficient enough not to require someone to talk to all the time during the day. However, the important thing is that you stay where you will be most comfortable and only you can decide that.

Mother had wanted you to come down to Gary for dinner on Monday evening, the 26th but we can easily arrange to go down there for dinner one of the nights that you are here. I plan to go down there for Christmas at the same time you leave here for Madison. I had planned on going to Milwaukee this Sunday but found that there will be no one dollar excursion this week. This wouldn't stop me except that if you are coming down Wednesday the interval will only be three days longer and if I can save some pennies I may be able to manage a Christmas present for you that would be more tangible and satisfactory than any fleeting visit I might make to Milwaukee. I also have a jury case to try Monday and after seeing you Sunday I should probably be unable to recall what the case was about, when appearing in court.

Please stop worrying, if you really are worrying, about what you may do to me, because the damage, if any, has already been done. Whatever you do, write to me, incoherently if you must, but anyway you can.

Bob

12. Milwaukee, Thursday [December 15, 1932]

Dear Bob,

It's growing harder each time I write to say anything to you because I am thinking so much. I only wish that my letters could give you the perfect satisfaction that yours give me.

The bit about love letters is swell. It's not only amusing but amazingly sound in its psychology. As for Greta's picture I conceitedly confess that I do see a resemblance, especially in the chin, but I do hope that you won't dwell on it enough to expect a Garbo when I next appear and be disappointed when you find only a waif.

20. Betty as Garbo?

I liked Westbrook Pegler, too, but I particularly liked the feeling it gave me that you think of me even during such a perfunctory performance as reading the morning paper.[50]

There was one thing I did not like about your letter. Why do you speak of giving me a tangible Christmas present when you have already given me a more tangible one than I have ever received, not to mention some very intangible ones? Just because I accept with apparent casualness a string of pearls doesn't mean that I am not genuinely thrilled with them. It means that like all Kehlers I am unable to express any but my most superficial emotions. I am serious when I say that any other gift would really embarrass me, especially since my imagination is so limited that I am unable to think of any gift that would really please you.

I have never had so much fun reading anything as I have "The Autobiography of Frank Lloyd Wright". I can hardly wait to get home at night. Your father and I are wallowing in sentimentality together. The whole thing is so overlaid with its relationship to the experiences and enthusiasms of my own childhood, my memories of Madison, the brief but pleasant ones of the Spring

---

[50] Bob had also enclosed a clipping of a Westbrook Pegler column from the *Chicago Daily Tribune*, a satirical account of the "sport" of biscuit tossing at formal banquets, "They're Eating Those Banquet Biscuits Now, Where Are the Old Roll Tossers? (New York, Dec. 12, Copyright 1932. By the *Chicago Tribune*). That enclosure has the following annotation in Bob's handwriting in the margin: "This will serve to introduce my principal excuse for buying the Tribune, Mr. Pegler, if you haven't already met him, and acquaint you with a sport I intend to take up after I perfect my snowball throwing."

Green country and above all with the fact that for me it is simply a book about you.[51]

You can easily see how disgustingly sentimental I am. This letter is full of it but I can't seem to help it.

I don't know whether another letter will make it easier or harder for me to wait until I see you, but I want one immediately –

Betty

13. Milwaukee, Sunday [December 18, 1932]

Dear Bob –

I still don't think telegrams are a satisfactory substitute for letters though that was a rather nice one, mangled as usual by Western Union – so badly that I think you could easily sue them. On consideration of the fact that you have a jury trial tomorrow (which I hope will be very successful from your standpoint) I understand and appreciate the telegram.

I am surprised that I sounded sane and logical because I feel and have felt pleasantly insane for some time. On second thought "pleasantly" is much too dull a word for it. Write in your own adjective.

I might add that you may not find me as good a witness as you expected. After being held down by the inevitable restrictions of letter-writing I feel that I shall have a lot to volunteer when I see you in person.

That should be enough to dispose of the telegram. I meant to mention in my last letter that I am pleased at the prospect of meeting your mother and flattered by her arranging it. Or did you?

---

51 *An Autobiography* by Frank Lloyd Wright was first published in March 1932 by Longmans, Green, and Company of London, New York, and Toronto. An article announcing its imminent publication appeared on p. 1 of the *Chicago Daily Tribune* of Saturday March 26, 1932, titled "Frank Lloyd Wright Tells Life and Love." The article continues on p. 18, where there is also a review of the book titled "Critic Finds Wright's Book Amazing Story" with the subtitle "All Questions of His Life Are Answered." That page also has a full spread of pictures of Wright, Olgivanna Milanoff Wright, Mamah Borthwick Cheney, Wright with his and Olgivanna's young daughter Iovanna, Miriam Noel Wright, and Catherine Lee Wright. Thus while Wright undoubtedly wrote the book to attempt to improve his public image, the press was still feeding on the scandals of his love life. The articles and the pictures say that Wright was married four times, calling Mamah Borthwick his second wife, although the couple was never able to marry legally since Catherine refused to grant Wright a divorce until 1922.

I haven't heard a word from Stewart so I am taking his consent to my vacation plans for granted. May I count on you to arrange that I stay some place?

I expect to take the five o'clock train which arrives shortly before seven on Wednesday evening. If I change my plans I shall wire you.

I still sound sane and logical, I'm afraid, but don't let it confuse you. If I'm sane now then I have been insane for my previous twenty-two and a half years.

Betty

14. Milwaukee [Wednesday, December 28, 1932]

Dear Bob,

You had me a bit upset on that "L" platform.[52] I don't remember telling you that I intend to arrive in Chicago shortly before seven Thursday evening.

This promises to be a very pleasant two days' work. Van, the guy who is working with me, and I go off and sleep in one hour shifts. It's swell. If you don't understand please ask me about it Thursday.

I'm so glad that I have five more days with you. I refuse to think beyond that. Please take care of your cold now that you're rid of me. I'm going to teach you the technique of checking colds–

Betty

---

[52] The "L" is the elevated electric railway system, which still exists in Chicago. At the time, the electric North Shore Line between Milwaukee and Chicago connected directly with the "L." Greg Borzo's *The Chicago "L"* (Charleston SC, Chicago IL, Portsmouth NH, San Francisco CA: Arcadia Publishing, 2009) is a good reference work on this subject.

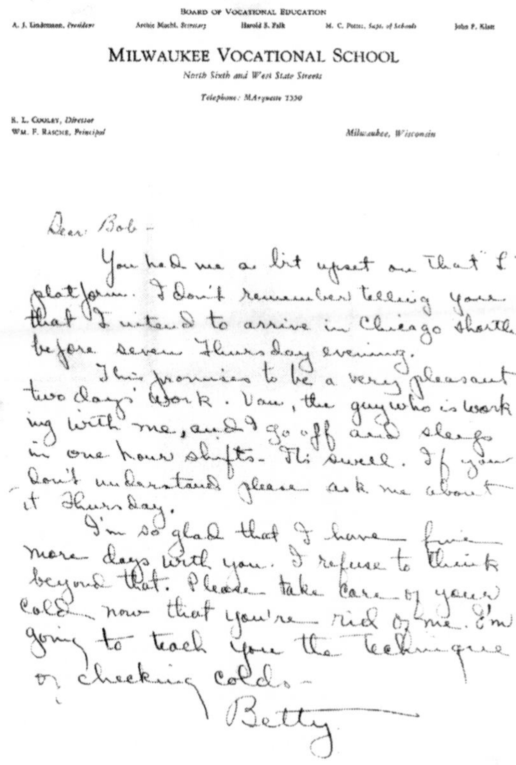
Board of Vocational Education

MILWAUKEE VOCATIONAL SCHOOL

North Sixth and West State Streets

Telephone: MArquette 7330

Milwaukee, Wisconsin

Dear Bob -

You had me a bit upset on that 'L' platform. I don't remember telling you that I intend to arrive in Chicago shortly before seven Thursday evening.

This promises to be a very pleasant two days' work. Van, the guy who is working with me, and I go off and sleep in one hour shifts. It's swell. If you don't understand please ask me about it Thursday.

I'm so glad that I have five more days with you. I refuse to think beyond that. Please take care of your cold now that you're rid of me. I'm going to teach you the technique of checking colds -

Betty

21. Letter No. 14, Milwaukee Vocational School stationery

15. Milwaukee, Tuesday [January 3, 1933]

Dear Bob -

There are special rates to Madison this weekend and I feel that I must go. You had better call Edris and tell her that I am not coming. I'm trying to be philosophic about existing without you for two weeks but it's damned hard.

I'm going to go at this business of trying to find a job in a much bigger way than I ever did when I graduated from college. I think I may be able to get a few suggestions from people in Madison and I am also going to write some friends of mine. I'd like to try places first where they might need a statistician because that's what I'd really like to do. I might get a break. I feel now that I could do anything successfully and that any number of people should want me in their business. That's the effect you have on me.

I don't suppose you will have a chance to talk to Stewart before he comes to Milwaukee but I shall anyway. I think he will be sympathetic and perhaps even helpful.

I'm falling asleep and can't write any more even in this dull, matter of fact vein.

There's really only one thing on my mind and in order that your documentary evidence may be as complete as mine, I'll write it. I love you.

Betty

Part Two: Engagement

Telling Family And Friends, Beginning To Search For A Job In Chicago For Betty

Letters 16–30, January 5–February 1, 1933

16. Chicago, Thursday [January 5, 1933]

Dear Betty,

Why is it that when you write me a letter on Tuesday I don't get it until Thursday? Do you carry them around and forget to mail them?[53] When I didn't hear from you yesterday I nearly telephoned you to reassure myself about you but your letter settled my doubts today.

If you must go to Madison I suppose that this week-end can be sacrificed as well as any and I called Edris in accordance with your request. I don't know whether or not you got the clipping I mailed, as you didn't mention it, but don't think I'm not serious about getting you a job here. I am putting everyone I know to work on the problem and hope the law of averages will yield some results. Mr. Peters is of course looking for a job anyway and has promised to look for you at the same time but he has so far not put forth much effort in this direction, even for himself. I even have Bentley working on this proposition. I might add that I have advanced the Chicago job idea to these people as mine rather than yours, so you need feel no embarrassment. When people ask me what you can do I tell them that you are an excellent statistician but are also a very bright girl and catch on fast at anything.

Perhaps your ex-professors and the people you worked for at Madison can put you in touch with somebody at Chicago or Northwestern who is familiar with whatever opportunities for statistical work may exist here. This insistence on finding you employment here certainly makes me feel like a parasitical marriage prospect but if my law practice doesn't produce more income than it ever has before, it certainly won't be because I haven't redoubled my efforts to

---

53 Betty's letters are often in envelopes postmarked the day after she wrote them.

make it do so. The more I think about it the surer I become that we must get married within a reasonable time, come what may, but we might as well exhaust what common sense we have left first in an effort to build a foundation for a completely successful marriage. If half the things they say about the power of love are true it's a cinch.

Bob

17. Milwaukee, Thursday [January 5, 1933]

Dear Bob -

I enjoyed your annotated edition of the Tribune want ads very much. You're a bit fresh, of course, considering the fact that you've known me only four months but I'll try to overlook that. Also - if clippings are merely a ruse to avoid writing letters don't think you can get away with that. I want both - and everything else I can get, as you may have noticed. Which leads me to inform you that I meant to ask you politely for your Deke pin[54] when I last saw you and shall when I see you again. After all, I only have a string of pearls, a radio and a sweater and a girl needs something tangible. Sometime if you wish I'll tell you why I refused it, because I think it's amusing. I don't want to write it for fear you'll misunderstand.

I just had dinner with Stewart and told him all. I had a very pleasant and profitable talk with him for about two hours. He approves highly, thinks you're a swell guy and a safe financial prospect. He has the same impression that I have: namely, that you know very definitely what you want and have the intelligence to get it. He also told me how much other people in Chicago like and admire you. I already knew that and I could love you without it but it gratified me nevertheless.

He went on to review for me in a nice and not too serious way the faults of the Kehlers in general and myself in particular and the various ways in which I am liable to make you and myself unhappy. I recognize the truth of all he said and am accordingly forearmed. I hope someone does the same for you.

You might be interested in knowing that I received a present on account of you today, in spite of the fact that I'm not engaged. I told my friend Margaret

---

[54] Bob was a member of the "Deke" (Delta Kappa Epsilon) fraternity while at Cornell.

Cooley[55] last night that I intend to marry you. (I hope you don't resent that. I don't tell everyone I see.) She appeared today with a broad grin and a very lovely pair of pajamas remarking characteristically that she liked to see all her friends married and that she wanted to do her bit toward making me go through with it - or words to that effect - which is her way of masking a friendly and generous impulse and amusing herself at the same time. At any rate her sense of humor nets me a pair of pajamas.

At this point I want to say something which I may not be able to express satisfactorily. I am writing what comes into my mind at random and hoping that you will interpret it as it is meant. At the same time I am afraid that I may sound a little smug and possessive because of the fact that you have asked me to marry you. I don't mean to be nor do I feel that way. I am much too apt to assume that you know how I feel because it is hard for me to express myself. I think you are absolutely right in not considering us engaged. That's a bad sentence but the idea is there. I meant to assure you, and do now, that I consider you as free as you feel I should be and that I don't want you to limit your social life in any way. I think on the contrary that it will be better for both of us if we do not. It certainly will not injure my emotional security in any way nor should it yours.

I set a very good example for you yesterday by staying home and killing an incipient case of the flu. I take pleasure in the fact that in some small problems of life I am more intelligent than you. In all seriousness I hope that you are being careful. I am more concerned about you than you think.

I could probably go on forever in my youthful introspective way but I feel that I have given you enough to misinterpret for one day. Not that I feel misunderstood but that letters are inevitably misinterpreted. Nevertheless I shall be very happy to misinterpret any you may care to write and as in the past shall probably do so to your very great advantage.

Betty

---

55 Margaret Cooley, the daughter of R. L. Cooley, the founder and head of the Milwaukee Vocational School, was Betty's college friend who helped her get her job there.

18. Chicago [Monday, January 9, 1933]

Bob sends no letter, but he does send a partial clipping from a newspaper:

SITUATIONS WANTED—FEMALE

(under "Professions and Trades," the following ad is outlined in black):

STATISTICIAN DESIRES WORK IN CHICAGO; now employed elsewhere; experienced in vocational studies and educational work. Address B 231 Tribune

Handwritten on back:

On the other side is an [*sic*] cl ad I ran for you, or rather us, in the Tribune today. Not one chance in a thousand of getting any replies but it's worth a trial even at those odds.

SITUATIONS WANTED—FEMALE.

Bookkeepers and Clerks.

A1 BKKPR.-STENO.—6 YRS. EXP. AUTOmobile line; excellent ref. Seeley 4932.

BKKPR.-SECY.-STENOG.—9 YEARS' EXP.; capable; best refs. Spaulding 5036.

RECEPTIONIST—OFF. WORK, CAN TAKE dicta.; $6 wk. Address C 358, Tribune.

SEVERAL YRS.' EXP. AS AUDITOR, BKPR., cashier, and office mgr. Whitehall 4380.

STENO.-BKKPR.—EXP. ACCTS. OFC.; N. W. univ. tr.; reas. sal. Prospect 7264.

Professions and Trades.

PER. POSITION, POWER SEW. MACHINE on leather goods; wk. work. Oak. 5908.

STATISTICIAN DESIRES WORK IN CHIcago; now employed elsewhere; experienced in vocational studies and educational work. Address B 231, Tribune.

Domestics and Cooks.

COL. WORKING GIRLS' CLUB—1ST-CLASS cooks, laundresses; genl. hsewk.; maids; clean'g; serving. Call Miss Mason. Oak. 7314.

22a. Clipping of classified ad Bob ran for Betty in the Chicago Tribune

22b. Bob's message on back of clipping of classified ad

19. Milwaukee, Monday [January 9, 1933]

Dear Bob –

I don't know why you don't get my letters sooner, but I'll try to mail them earlier and see if that helps.

I appreciated your telegram. You may wake me up that way any time you wish.

Mother sends you her regards. She's a little doubtful about it all. That's her nature. I think I managed to convince her that yours is a sterling character and that I'm not going to do anything rash. In the course of my conversations about you I told her that I had formed a fairly objective estimate of your faults as well as your virtues during my early acquaintance with you. She immediately evinced great interest in your faults and I had a hell of [a] time thinking of any.

Who has been giving you advice? I'm curious to know.

I stayed at the office tonight and wrote three letters to people at the university who may be able to help me get a job. You may make something of me yet, Bob. I haven't felt so ambitious since I was a junior in college and wanted to reorganize our economic system. I have never felt so adventurous – by which I mean the feeling of wanting to risk my present existence for the sake of something infinitely better.

Please don't ever talk about being a parasitic marriage prospect. I know that you are working for me. Why shouldn't I be equally eager to work for you? The only reason I have for wanting a job in Chicago is so that I may marry you. There will be advantages and disadvantages for us both if I do achieve it. It certainly means as much to me as to you.

I intend to come to Chicago this weekend probably arriving at three on Saturday. I shall write Edris tonight and you might call her also if it's convenient. I hope she will be able to have me.

Now that this weekend is past I feel that I actually am going to see you soon. I have missed you so terribly and I have so many things to talk to you about –

Betty

20. Chicago [Wednesday] Jan 11, 1933 [sent Special Delivery]

Dear Betty,

Apparently a letter can't be mailed in Milwaukee one day and reach Chicago the next. Yours came today and I am pleased to receive your mother's regards. She is apparently holding herself well in check. I am afraid that I am too concerned with my own feelings toward you to worry much about those of your family toward me but I wish you could contrive some way to break the news to Gordon[56] which would induce him to write me a letter; preferably one which would make the one Stewart got seem like a gay revelation of his lighter self.

Regardless of how well you may have convinced your mother to the contrary you are going to do something rash when you marry me. I hope you never do anything rasher. And you are going to marry me with or without a job in Chicago or Milwaukee or anywhere else, even if we can't live together more than twenty-four hours, if you feel as I do about it. What we are doing now is simply going through the motions of removing some of the rash features from the act by attempting to establish a reasonably sound economic basis for it but I

---

[56] Gordon was Betty's oldest brother, ten years older than she.

am afraid that, from your side, it can hardly be regarded as a rational one under any conditions. Love appears to have made a gambler of you but the effect on me, naturally inclined to gamble, has simply been to reduce all gambles concerning you to sure things. If this isn't quite clear to you I doubt whether it is to me either.

Enclosed is a response to the ad I ran for you. Acting as your manager, I called Mr. Pugh on the phone and learned that the work he has in mind has no salary attached, compensation being entirely on a royalty basis, but you can do it in your spare time wherever you care to work. His company is the F.A. Davis Co. of Philadelphia, about which you may be able to learn something from Dr. Cooley. He also claims to know people at your school so you might ask about him there. Inasmuch as his letter is scarcely a mash note I don't think it would do any harm to talk to him. I'll call him again and make an appointment for Saturday afternoon unless I hear from you to the contrary. There are a number of other employment possibilities that I want to discuss with you when you get here.

[At the start of the second sheet] Please note that I am not given to stingy, one sheet letters. It was disappointing to learn that you aren't coming down until Saturday afternoon as I was counting the hours till Friday night and will now have to add twenty more. However, it may be well to save the Saturdays for later on when you may have to be here on Saturday mornings for interviews regarding jobs. There I go again - putting you to work. If you do get a job before you marry me I shall probably end up by staying at home - writing a novel or something—while you work your fingers to the bone supporting me.

My business is much better to the extent that I have had a lot to do lately but for some reason I don't seem to have much money. I shall give the money situation some attention before the end of the week.

Please don't ever say "I may marry you" again.

Bob

21. Milwaukee, Monday [January 16, 1933]

Dear Bob -

This is going to be a poor sort of a letter for I've written two before this and I'm asleep at the desk.

I answered the "greeter" ad this afternoon and I'm anxious to see whether I get a reply. I mentioned everything I could think of except my age.[57]

Tomorrow night when I've recovered from my weekend with you I'm going to start the application letter. Even though I am sleepy I have come back as usual with renewed optimism and mental energy. When two such smart and pleasant people as we want anything so badly we ought to be able to get it.

Even though we do disapprove of sentimentality in letters I'm unable to avoid it altogether. I love you immeasurably more each minute I'm with you and don't see how it's possible. When I compare my emotions now to those I had when I accepted your generous offer to marry me it seems that it was almost a marriage of convenience I was plotting. Now you know how full of guile I am.

It has just occurred to me that you gave Celeste Horton your home phone, or didn't you? She certainly won't be calling you at night.

I just wrote the girl whom I forgot to call so that's all right. It was only important as a friendly gesture and not from a business standpoint anyway and I'm not going to be dumb.

Edris gave us some good advice which I must tell you some time unless you're tired of hearing advice. We have plenty of time to act on it anyway.

My letter is dribbling off into nothingness, I fear. I'll try to write you a nice, bright one tomorrow.

Betty

22. Milwaukee, Tuesday [January 17, 1933]

Dear Bob -

I really haven't much to write you about that I want to say in a letter but it's the only thing I can think of to do for you.

The application letter I sent to the emergency welfare was returned tonight - wrong address - so I am sending it to Jean so that she can locate the woman. I'm rather disappointed about that. I was anxious to see what the reply would be.

---

[57] In the *Chicago Daily Tribune* of January 15, 1933, under WANTED—FEMALE HELP, I found the following ad, which appears to be the one Betty answered: "WOMAN—OVER 28: RECEPTIONIST; CAP-able greeter. Address, B 582. Tribune." Betty was twenty-two years old at the time of the letter.

If we could decide whether I am coming to Chicago or you to Milwaukee it would be nice. I imagine Mary might make other plans if I told her you weren't coming. Also please let me know if you should find it's important for me to try to get Saturday off. There's a chance Pat might go away on Friday in which case it would be all right for me to ask him before he goes. I don't think we ought to waste it, however.

Mary has worked the last two nights so Porter (her husband) and I have been playing ping pong. I'm still lousy but trying to improve before I play with you again. I've told Porter you can take him so you'd better be good if you come to Milwaukee again.

I'm going to "The Good Earth" tomorrow night so that I can argue with you. That discussion made me feel that it might be worth seeing.[58]

The days go slowly without you. Thank God it's only one week I have to wait this time. Try to write me at least once before I see you, won't you? No - you don't have to do that unless you happen to because I know you're doing much more important things for me. Consider that unsaid.

There's a melancholy tone to my letter but there shouldn't be - lonely or not, I have more to be happy about than I ever had in my life before.

Betty

23. Chicago, [Thursday] Jan 19, 1933 [sent Special Delivery]

Dear Betty,

Your letters this week have excited me more than I can say. I have almost begun to believe that you love me of your own volition rather than as a mere response to the pressure in that direction that I have tried to exert. It has of course been impossible, for some time, for me to contemplate any future existence without you and the longer the present separation, with spasmodic contacts, continues, the more unendurable it becomes. However, Saturday and Sunday should bring some solace.

---

[58] The Theater Guild's dramatization of Pearl S. Buck's controversial novel about life in China, *The Good Earth*, is reviewed favorably in the *Chicago Daily Tribune* on January 1, 1933 by Charles Collins. *The Milwaukee Journal* of Sunday, January 15, 1933, announces the opening of the play at Milwaukee's Pabst Theatre for a limited one-week engagement on Monday, January 16, and the production is favorably reviewed by Richard S. Davis in the same paper on Tuesday, January 17, 1933.

I called on Mr. Gardner today and learned that his job pays only twelve dollars a week. Moreover, he tells me he is looking for a girl who will smile at the customers in such a way that they will enjoy waiting in her presence to have their teeth extracted. There is no doubt about your being able to do this but I think a job where you might smile or frown, according to your feelings, might be more pleasant. Nothing else has developed here which would require your presence on Saturday so I will come to Milwaukee if that is convenient for Mary. If not wire me Saturday morning as to when you will arrive in Chicago.

Don't be discouraged about the job situation as we have really only just begun to work on it. I'll bring your bracelet with me and possibly some sketches for the ring.[59]

Bob

---

[59] See Illustration No. 23, the sketch for rings on Erik Magnussen letterhead, found filed with the courtship letters. Apparently Magnussen was a Danish artist with an independent spirit, not unlike Frank Lloyd Wright: "Erik Magnussen (1884-1960) was a self-taught silversmith, too independent to be accepted by any workshop. He was raised in an intellectual atmosphere and was apprenticed at 14 in his uncle's art gallery. He opened his own workshop in 1909, producing extraordinary naturalistic silver-gilt and porcelain brooches of insects for the Royal Copenhagen Porcelain Manufactory. In 1925, he moved to New York City and became artistic director for Gorham Silver Co. He worked independently from the other designers, producing modernistic pieces that were completely opposed to the traditional Colonial Gorham designs. This did not endear him to his fellow workers. (His radically geometric "Cubic" coffee set might have been created by a Russian Constructivist.) After the stock market crash of 1929, Magnussen left Gorham and opened his own shops in New York City and Chicago. When they went bankrupt, he maintained a shop in Hollywood to design for the stars.... (Ginger Moro, "Scandinavian Modern Jewelry: Denmark & Finland," *JCK-Jewelers Circular Keystone*, 11/1/1996. <http://www.jckonline.com/article/CA6253460.html>)."

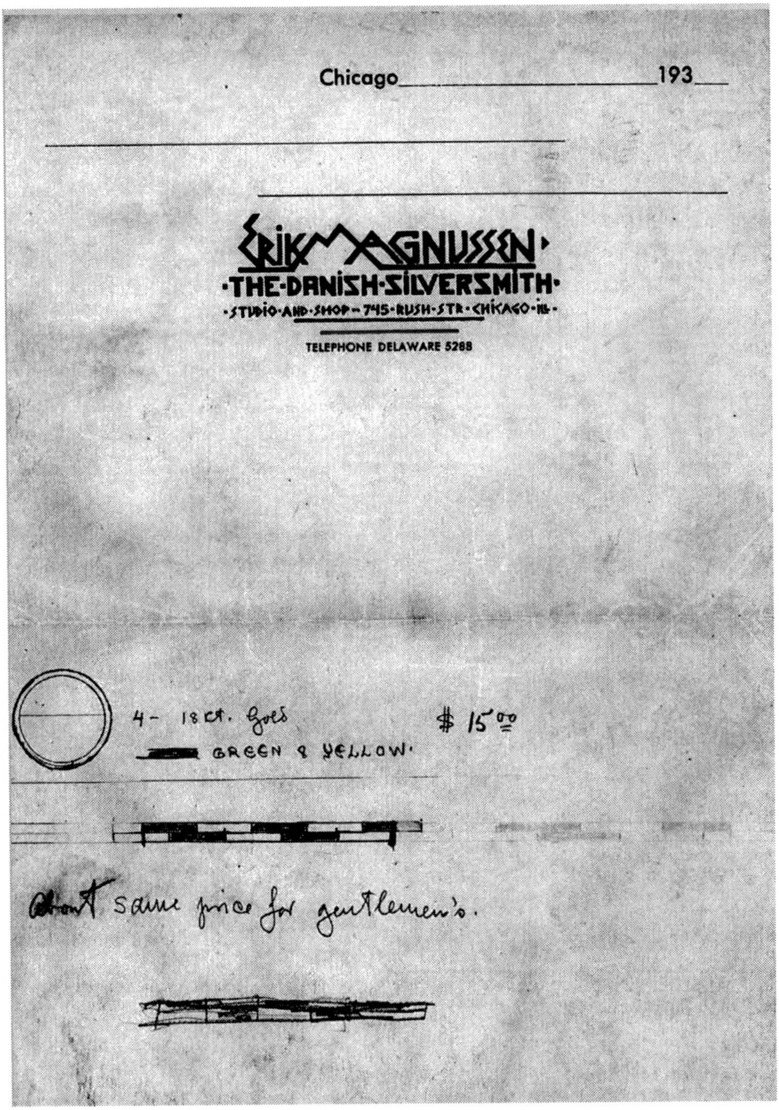

Chicago__________________ 193__

ERIK MAGNUSSEN
·THE·DANISH·SILVERSMITH·
·STUDIO·AND·SHOP·745·RUSH·STR·CHICAGO·ILL·
TELEPHONE DELAWARE 5288

4- 18 ct. Gold $15.00
GREEN & YELLOW.

About same price for gentlemen's.

23. Sketch for rings on Erik Magnussen letterhead

24. Milwaukee, Sunday [January 22, 1933?]—enclosed in an envelope with the date torn off

Dear Bob,

I'm starting another week with a flourish and I'll try not to fold this time. Last week's remark is still true - I love you more each time I'm with you. In your last letter you implied that only the sheer force of your personality kept me in love with you - I refuse to believe that I am dominated by you in that respect. There's really no use arguing by correspondence about love but I assure you that mine is a thing of my own and you couldn't stop it if you tried.

There's one quality of yours which I value more than anything else in you but when I try to describe it seems to be a hodge-podge of all the standard and sterling virtues such as understanding, sympathy, unselfishness, cooperation - I still haven't described it. With that one quality of yours I feel that if I do even half my share we can't fail to be happy. You have innumerable other good points almost as fascinating but I'm saving them for the rest of the week. Just to keep up your interest in seeing me again I'll tell you that I forgot to mention some of the most important advice that Edris gave me, which also concerns you. When we get down to the facts of life again I'll tell you.[60]

I've been thinking about my ring. I'm unable to supply a new idea but I wonder if your first one wasn't simpler and better than the last sketch. I'll attempt to draw it thus.[61] That of course is much too wide and the color variation too sensational but it seems to me that one alternation of color might be better than cutting it up so much. What do you think?

I'll try to get hold of a book keeping text tomorrow in preparation for next week.

Please don't worry about the future and don't think that I'm getting tired of you, consciously or unconsciously. You're all the future I want and I'm going to get you.

Betty

---

60 This is probably the advice about birth control from Edris that Betty mentions in her videotaped interviews.

61 In Betty's sketch (Illustration No. 24), the different colored bands in each row are not offset from each other, as in Magnussen's sketch (Illustration No. 23), but rather in a pattern where a plain band is directly over a dark one, and vice versa.

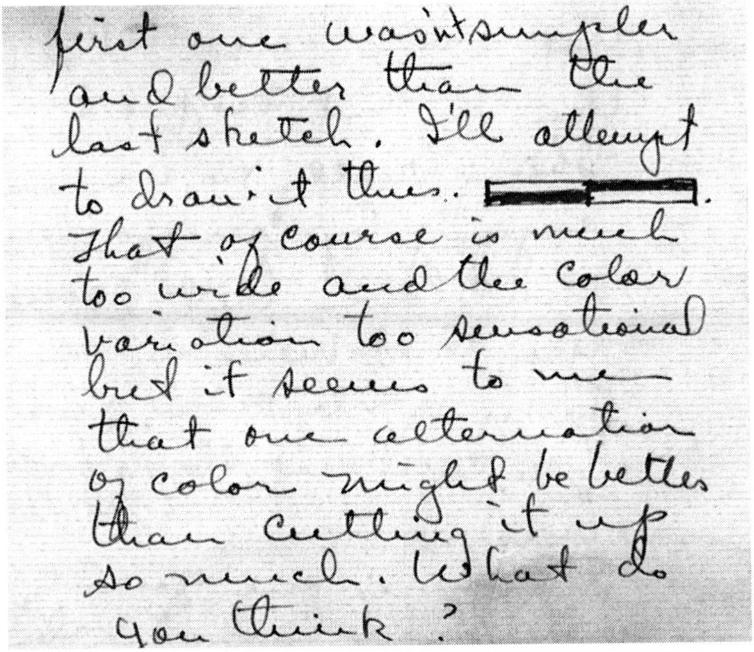
first one wasn't simpler and better than the last sketch. I'll attempt to draw it thus. That of course is much too wide and the color variation too sensational but it seems to me that one alternation of color might be better than cutting it up so much. What do you think?

24. Excerpt of Letter No. 24, with Betty's sketch for the ring

25. Milwaukee, Monday [January 23, 1933]

Dear Bob,

I'm almost afraid to write you tonight. I'm in such an insane state of mind that I know I'll aggravate your troubles rather than assuage them. I don't see how I'm going to be able to live without you much longer. I've not only lost all reason but all sense of humor. I can't be light about it. I want you and you're absolutely all I want. The hell of it for you is that I seem to wear myself out mentally and emotionally thinking of you every minute that you're gone and by the time I see you again I turn reasonable. Sometimes it seems to me that I fail you in every possible way. You're incredibly patient with me, I know.

I wonder if you don't have a profounder effect on the type of emotion I feel toward you than I was willing to admit last night. Do you suppose that if you had assured me that you didn't want to marry me until you had established a substantial fortune that I would be calm about it, too? Try it sometime. I'll probably burst into tears and beg you to marry me. I might even put myself into a compromising situation and entreat you to save my honor.

I know that I'm selfishly easing my feelings by writing you this way. Underneath I still feel that we must be rational to some extent for the sake of our mutual happiness. It's so damned hard to be rational when I know you're willing not to be.

It might help you to know that before my complete collapse of morale this evening I read two chapters of bookkeeping and it seems fairly easy. Mr. Winkel also knows a system which he recommends highly for the unskilled. It's a set of books with headings already made for all types of accounting plus non-technical explanations of how to go about each step. I'm going to look that over soon.

Please write me a sensible letter about how you regret that it's impossible for you to marry me right now. I may regain my balance if you do.

Just as an anticlimax may I add that I love you.

Betty

26. Milwaukee, Tuesday [January 24, 1933]

Dear Bob,

I don't know why I'm writing you every day unless it's just to impress you. I don't even think it's a good idea. It always seemed so silly to me when people wrote every day. What could they possibly have to say to each other? I guess the answer is still nothing of any importance. I'm still pretty unhappy about the general situation but I'm trying to get over it. I remind myself of a spoiled child whining because she can't have everything when she has almost everything. I'll try to cultivate a more courageous attitude and do something constructive about it.

I can't see how not seeing you so often will ever be a solution for any problem of ours. Just being with you makes me a new and better person. If it makes it easier for you, however, you know that I'll gladly do it.

I'm still studying my bookkeeping and it really fascinates me. I think I'd be a pretty good bookkeeper.

I'm going to a bridge party tonight. I don't want to go but I think the stupidest thing I can do is to stay home alone. You seem to have destroyed my self-sufficiency, temporarily, I hope. I'll certainly be a bore if I depend on you and being with you for my entire happiness after we're married. You'll knock that out of me anyway along with my other faults you are planning a campaign against.

I promise you that I won't write another letter this week unless I can write a more constructive one. It scares me a little to write into blank space and not know how you're reacting to my sobbing. I have apparently forgotten my convictions on the dangers of letter writing.

Tomorrow will be the middle of the week which always is a high point for me. It means I'm actually going to be with you soon.

Betty

27. Milwaukee, Wednesday [January 25, 1933]

Dear Bob,

My business correspondence is beginning to bear fruit but very sour fruit. I received today a letter from Professor Ingraham with the usual line, mentioning no people in Chicago whom I can see, and a letter from the Unemployment Relief stating that they are permitted to hire only legal residents of Illinois. I also received your telegram which wasn't sour except that you don't believe me which is probably all right. I've decided that you're kept so busy with my impassioned correspondence that you have no time to write me so this is the end for this week. Or else fitting your thoughts neatly into fifty words holds the same attraction for you as a jig-saw or cross-word puzzle.

That reminds me that I won a jig-saw puzzle as first prize at bridge last night. Are you proud of me?

Mr. Patterson has given me this Saturday off on condition that I am present next Saturday when most everyone will be away. I feel that I have to take it this week or not at all. It's up to you to see that I have someone important to see next Saturday and no one the next Saturday. Do you think you can manage that?

Unless you have some other suggestion to make I shall take the six o'clock train arriving at Grand Avenue about eight on Friday evening. I shall have my dinner before I come.

The Milwaukee Journal is starting a series of articles on ping pong. They say it's an excellent way to reduce the waistline which certainly arouses my interest to a fever pitch.

Will you please ask Edris again if it's convenient for me to stay with her? I'd rather not write her this time.

Betty

28. Chicago, Thursday 1 A.M. [January 26, 1933; sent Special Delivery]

Dear Betty,

Stop wasting your money on telephone calls, particularly when I'm not here. It's a delightful habit but an expensive one. I was playing bridge with George Miller, who works for the telephone company and has lined up a girl for you to talk to there. However, she doesn't ordinarily work on Saturday so you probably won't be able to see her this week-end.

Will meet you Friday night at Grand Avenue at eight o'clock and wish it were seven. You can stay with Edris providing that all advice given to you is promptly passed on to me.

Please relax? If you behave the way you have been writing I don't know what will become of us. I don't anyway, so it probably doesn't make any difference, but it really isn't fair to work on me that way while you're safely out of reach. Try talking that way this week-end and see what happens to you.

Seriously, regardless of how gratifying it may be to me to feel that you are upset about the present rather helpless condition of our love for each other there is no sense in your torturing yourself about it. I know that you love me and you know that I love you. Obviously the next step is to see that that love culminates in marriage to each other and to try and surround that marriage with circumstances that will permit us to live and be happy together. That must necessarily be done calmly and with some suppression of emotional excitation.

You seem to have become radical and I conservative but I hope it won't be necessary for me to remain conservative to preserve your radicalism. This is nonsense. What I want is to see and touch you; maybe even talk to you.

Bob

29. Chicago [Tuesday, January 31, 1933][62]

Dear Betty,

Enclosed is an ad for you to answer that I clipped from tonight's Daily News - the University girl, not the Girl-German 20-40.[63] Answering these things may seem silly to you and the chances are one hundred to one against any of them producing a suitable job but it is the only way to put the law of averages to work for you.

Miss Johnson is still sick and you are reading my own typing, which [ic written over ci] until [t written over c] I wrote the which was errorless.I love you.I love you.I love you.Not nearly as good practice as Now is the time for all good men to come to the aid of the party.I missed the double space because I was disconcerted to find no exclamation mark on this typewriter.Do you know whether they have them or whether you make one with a single punctuation mark and a period like [i written over o] this!Not bad.I love you!Excellent.Please destroy this when received as~~m~~ I have a few things I want to do, such as getting married, before they put me in an asylum.What you should insist on is not a physical [y written over s] but a mental examination.

Bob [handwritten][64]

---

62 The letter is typewritten, double-spaced, with no spaces after periods, on Bob's business letterhead. See Illustration No. 25.

63 The enclosure was not found with the letters, but in the *Chicago Daily News* of Tuesday, January 31, 1933, under HELP WANTED—FEMALE, Offices, Stores, Etc., I found the following ad: "UNIVERSITY girl—For office. age; salary, religion. Address D H 199. Daily News." Right under it, under the heading "Domestic Help" is: "GIRL—German 20-40; gen. hswk; exp'd; priv. room; Christian family; $6. Midway 6219."

64 On the same day, Bob sent a handwritten letter to his father announcing his engagement to Betty (WO67B07, Frank Lloyd Wright archive, copyright @The Frank Lloyd Wright Foundation 1990). His father replied on February 15 wishing Llewellyn luck and offering the couple a "chapel wedding and dinner here at Taliesin" and a honeymoon in the area if they wished (WO67C09, Frank Lloyd Wright archive, copyright @The Frank Lloyd Wright Foundation 1990).

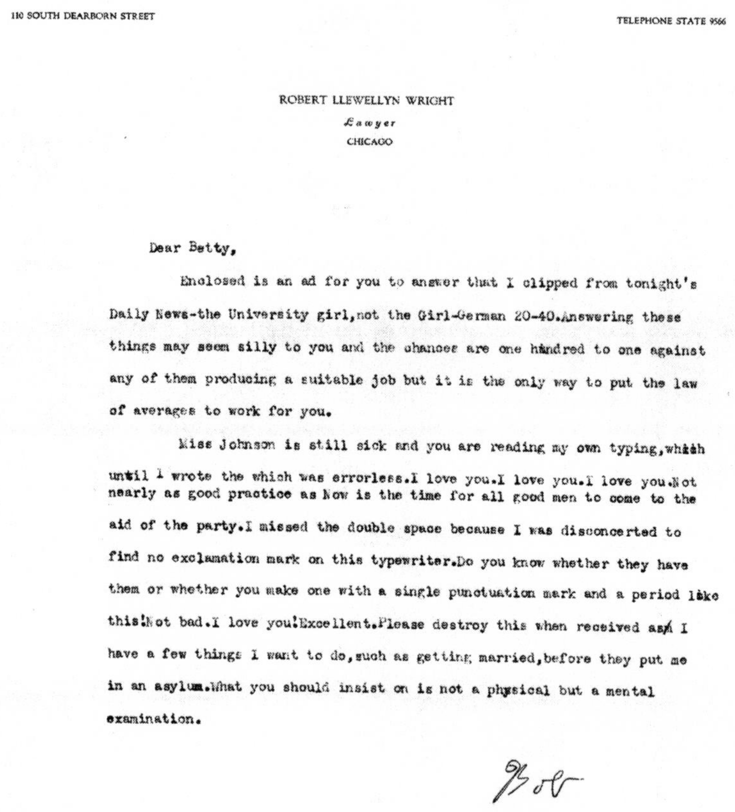

110 SOUTH DEARBORN STREET

TELEPHONE STATE 9566

ROBERT LLEWELLYN WRIGHT
Lawyer
CHICAGO

Dear Betty,

Enclosed is an ad for you to answer that I clipped from tonight's Daily News-the University girl,not the Girl-German 20-40.Answering these things may seem silly to you and the chances are one hundred to one against any of them producing a suitable job but it is the only way to put the law of averages to work for you.

Miss Johnson is still sick and you are reading my own typing,which until I wrote the which was errorless.I love you.I love you.I love you.Not nearly as good practice as Now is the time for all good men to come to the aid of the party.I missed the double space because I was disconcerted to find no exclamation mark on this typewriter.Do you know whether they have them or whether you make one with a single punctuation mark and a period like this!Not bad.I love you!Excellent.Please destroy this when received as I have a few things I want to do,such as getting married,before they put me in an asylum.What you should insist on is not a physical but a mental examination.

Bob

25. *Letter No. 29, in Bob's typing*

30. Milwaukee, Wednesday [February 1, 1933]

Dear Bob,

Your letter disorganized me today for a full hour - but do it again, please. It relieves me so much to have you appear as insane as I feel and act, and you've never been really insane in a letter before. Mad as I have seemed in some of my letters I have never dared to write as madly as I think.

I answered the ad of course. It sounds like a fairly good lead to me, if there weren't so many of us University girls. There's one thing to be said for the ad method - there is at least a job open which is more than can be said for most of the places we think of.

I spent a quiet and healthful evening at the Y.W.C.A., which is certainly better than a speakeasy.[65] I bowled two sloppy games and then went to my mental hygiene class which was pretty good tonight. I think I'll adopt that for my Wednesday evening routine. Mens sana in corpore sano - it fits in so neatly that I had to write it.

You'd better write me where you want me to meet you at three Saturday or at seven minutes to three if I must be exact. There's a slight possibility of my arriving at two, but very slight. You might plan, however, to be available at that time and also at three.

Your typing is certainly as lousy as any I've ever seen. Your only possible basis for criticism of me is that I am a woman (or nearly one) and should be able to do those small things well. There are no exclamation points on any standard keyboard but with your never-failing intelligence you worked out the correct solution.

I love you with such sentimental hysteria that I am tempted to put crosses at the bottom of my letter. I won't. There's only one way to show you that I do love you, and I'll employ that next Saturday.

Betty

P.S. Will you tell Edris definitely that I'm coming?

---

65 "Speakeasies," unlicensed establishments dispensing alcoholic beverages, had been present in the United States from at least the 1890s. They flourished and became immensely popular during the Prohibition era (1920-1933), when the sale, manufacture and transportation of alcohol were illegal. Bartenders would tell patrons to "speak easy" (speak quietly) when ordering so as not to arouse suspicion. <http://www.answers.com/topic/speakeasy#References>

Part Three: Doubts And Struggle

Can We Make It Financially? Who Should Support Whom? Can Love Conquer All?

Letters 31–110, February 7–May 29, 1933

31. Milwaukee, Tuesday [February 7, 1933]

Dear Bob -

Are you having a blizzard, too?[66] I'm so excited I can scarcely contain myself. School was closed early this afternoon. It's just like the day when Stewart carried me to kindergarten on his back which has always ranked as one of the high points in my life.

This is one of the times I wish that I lived with someone, preferably you. I have books, magazines, jigsaw puzzles, cigarets *[sic]* - all the requisites for a comfortable evening at home except food and you. I might even waive the food for tonight. Why couldn't this happen when I was in Chicago so that I couldn't get to Milwaukee?

I feel that I was childish and selfish in my attitude last weekend and I'll try not to be that way again. I've been that way before and said that before also but I mean it this time. It's ridiculous of me to put pressure on you that way when I know you love me and are doing everything possible to marry me. It's selfish of me, too, to stick to the point that we must be together in order to get married. On second thought that does seem necessary. What I am trying to say is this. If in three months I haven't a job in Chicago and you haven't adequate income to support me I'm not going to become a burden to you. In that case I

---

66 The blizzard is a front-page story in *The Milwaukee Journal* for February 7, 1933: "The blinding snowstorm, which began Monday night, will continue unabated through Tuesday and the city will awake Wednesday morning to find the temperature 12 below zero, probably more snow falling and the wind blowing strongly from the northwest. Whipped by a wind of gale proportions, the snowfall which began at 6:05 p.m. Monday continued Tuesday. The snow filled the air until at times it was difficult to see across a narrow street. The snow at a temperature a few degrees above zero remained hard and dry. By 2 p.m. it was estimated by the weather bureau the total fall since Monday night was more than 11 inches."

think we ought to get married and live apart, or at least we ought to consider it seriously.

I hope you've gone to see the ring. I want very much to hear what you think of it. If you like it I'm quite sure I will.

I'm sitting here trying to think of some way to tell you how wonderful you are. That's a disgustingly sentimental statement but my thought is not quite that bad. It's just that your reactions in any situation are so utterly satisfying to me. You're the most constructively sympathetic person I've ever known. I wish I could do something large and impressive to show you how much I appreciate it. I feel very earnest about it. Boy, could I cook and bear children if that would help you! You would want [the rest is written up the side of the page] me to produce an income instead which I don't seem to be able to do right now. I'll do that first, though, and I'll promise not to bear children --

Betty

32. Chicago [Wednesday] Feb. 8, 1933

Dear Betty,

There is nothing like a basement to give a feeling of complete security in a blizzard.[67] We are not snow-bound but that is the fault of the janitor's prodigious snow-shovelling. If you were here I'm sure we could be comfortable together and never miss the twin-beds I must pry loose from John[68] and if we aren't going to live together soon I am less human than I feel. If we can't arrange our finances so that we can do so all the time then we can at least do so on week-ends, which, according to some of our advanced thinkers, is an arrangement more conducive to happy married life than constant contact. However, I am enough of a skeptic to want to test the theory by constant and unremitting contact for an indefinite, or better, infinite period of time and agree with you that we ought to first put in two or three months intensive effort toward making that experiment (?) possible.

---

[67] The *Chicago Daily Tribune* for Wednesday, February 8, 1933, has a full page of pictures of the blizzard (p. 26) with the headline "Sub-Zero Temperatures Sweep into Chicago on Heels of Heavy Snowfall—Schools to Remain Closed Today."

[68] John was the second oldest of Bob's older brothers, born in 1892. See n. 88.

Jim Cunningham reports that no applications are even being considered at present by the Cook County Bureau of Public Welfare so that is out. I am having Mother write a letter of introduction for you to Miss Bennett, who is the female hirer for the World's Fair[69] but I don't think they are doing any hiring at present.

Do you have a holiday on the 13th as the banks and schools do here[?]. If so we ought to get in a two day week-end.[70] Even if you come down here I would prefer to pay the rail fare as it is certainly my turn to make the trip. If the city is going to stop paying you you had better start saving now, anyway.

I haven't seen the ring but will stop in there before the end of the week. If you can conveniently be at home between ten and eleven Friday night I'll try and call you then. In the meantime don't think about such mundane things as cooking, bearing children and producing income. All I want from you is the only thing I can offer you at the moment – love.

Bob

33. Milwaukee, Wednesday [February 8, 1933]

Dear Bob,

Mrs. Mills says she will let you stay here Saturday for a buck, so if you think it advisable and it appeals to you [you] can come here instead of my coming to Chicago. I agree with you in thinking I had better not come there unless it's important in a business way. If you'd rather just come for Sunday or if you think it wise to skip this weekend altogether that's all right, too. I of course want to see you as I always do but I can stand it this time.

I hope that your cold is all right by this time but I have a feeling you're sick again. I can't wait to work on those colds with my superior health technique. I'm interested in it for my sake as well as yours.

I have nothing to report to you at the moment.

---

69 The "Century of Progress Exhibition," or "World's Fair," took place on Chicago's Lakefront and Northerly Island from May 27 to Nov. 12, 1933. While it didn't help Betty get a job, it was considered "a boost for both the local economy and the city's morale" (*World's Fairs* by Erik Mattie [New York: Princeton Architectural Press, 1998], 161–62).

70 The *Chicago Daily Tribune* for Monday, February 13, 1933, has a headline: "Banks, Markets, Schools Pause for Lincoln Day."

Please let me know about the weekend as soon as you decide yourself. The only reason I don't like to have you come to Milwaukee is that I feel the expense is too great for you. If you'd let me do something occasionally I'd feel better about that. I do think we have a better time in Chicago, too, but that's because I'm not as resourceful as you. I'll try to be more so if you come this time.

Love, Betty

34. Milwaukee, Monday [February 13, 1933]

Dear Bob,

It's snowing again and I haven't you here to get you snowbound. I'll do it yet, though, or get you sick and keep you here - anything to get you in my power.

It was so nice of you to come this weekend and I had such a swell time, though it wasn't very exciting for you, I'm afraid. You've cured me completely. I hardly coughed a cough all day long.

You seemed just a trifle discouraged this time about the future and I don't want you to feel that way even for a day. There's more than one way of solving our problem and if we can't achieve ideal conditions immediately we will eventually. I am so happy to have you even as I have you now, and I want you to feel that way about it, too.

I am assuming that I will come to Chicago next weekend. If you see any objection to that please tell me. I'll do my best not to bother Edris and if possible to make it easier for her. If you should see Stewart you might ask him whether he thinks I am imposing on her too much. He should be able to judge and he'll tell you, I know.

Tell me whether you get this letter on Tuesday or Wednesday. I have a theory that it arrives the next day if I mail if before dinner, and I should like to have that checked.

I am having the New Yorker sent to you because you've been such a good boy of late. I can of course have it stopped at any time if your behavior is not satisfactory. I am hoping this method will be so effective that I shall not have to install locks on the doors.

Please eat enough and get a lot of sleep before I see you again, so that I won't feel conscience stricken at having kept you here past your bedtime -

Betty

P.S. Please excuse the envelope trouble.[71] The supply is low.

35. Chicago, [Tuesday] Feb. 14, 1933

Dear Betty,

Your gift to me of the New Yorker makes my fifteen cent valentine look cheap but is very encouraging because it looks as though you are planning on moving in. Anyway, it will save me fifteen cents a week from now on.

I'm glad to hear that your cough is cured. I expect to have you here for the week-end and will make the necessary arrangements with Edris. She has had my dictionary for nearly a week so feel no compunctions about asking her favors.

The Shore line train outdid itself and made the trip in two hours and twenty minutes and I didn't get up until nine o'clock so I got as much sleep as you did Sunday night. I saw Stewart for a few minutes last night, just long enough to accuse him of neglecting you during your recent illness, which I assured him was very serious, but I wasn't credible enough to move him.

I haven't much in mind for you in the way of job hunting this week-end, although Bud Kuchsted is reporting a possible opening with a firm that makes a clothes line that requires no clothes-pins, with which he has just associated himself. However, the ring problem will require a great deal of attention, so get here as soon as possible. In the meantime you might tell me you love me.

Bob

36. Milwaukee, Wednesday [February 15, 1933]

Dear Bob,

I have just read your very nice letter and I'm afraid it will result in a flood of sentimentality. I don't like to make an ass of myself, you know, but after your closing remark I have to confess that it's only by a stern effort of will that I manage to keep "I love you" out of every paragraph I write you and every sentence I speak to you. I think it a hundred times a day and even wake up in the middle of the night positively aching to tell you again that I love you. And even though it's all I think of it's such a damned pale phrase for what I feel.

---

[71] The envelope appears to have another name written on it and then erased off, taking the surface off the paper.

See what you've done – I'm so disorganized now that I can't settle down to the ordinary topics of correspondence.

You've made it a very nice week so far with your valentine yesterday and a letter today, when I usually don't hear from you at all until Thursday. The valentine delighted me especially. It made me feel that I am arousing a creative spark in you which will undoubtedly make your life richer. Incidentally you certainly don't need to feel chagrined because upon receiving it I was rather sad at not having sent you one. The other was something I had planned to do for a long time.

You keep right on getting Edris indebted to you so that I can visit her constantly. I think it's a great idea. I played bridge last night, very badly as usual. I promise to concentrate on it after we're married, but how can I remember anything so trivial when my thoughts keep wandering to you all the time I'm playing?

Don't ever make a remark like that again. If you have half the intuition I've always thought you display you would know that every time I write I'm trying to tell you, without boring you with repetition, that I love you --

Betty

[written up the side of the page]: P.S. I'm afraid I can't make it before 2:53 this weekend – I'll be at Grand Avenue then – I love you – B.

37. Milwaukee, Thursday [February 16, 1933]

Dear Bob –

I can scarcely settle down to writing you tonight I feel so good – or should it be well? I hate to feel energetic like this when you're not here. It seems such a waste of a good mood –

Someone passed a clipping around the office yesterday which made me feel very optimistic. It related the finds of a survey on the incomes in professional and skilled occupations. Doctors and lawyers were highest, the lawyers earning an average of over $5000 a year. Think what we'll do with that in a few years' time. Nothing could make me believe that you're not way above average in legal ability so that should mean much more for us. I'm on the point of deciding what colleges our six children should go to – anyway, aside from such foolishness, I think you're a smart guy, and I'm even willing to admit that a doctor's degree surpasses a Phi Beta Kappa key.[72]

Danny Jones just called me up and passed remarks about driving me to Chicago Saturday. I don't think he's serious but if he is it will save me money. He understands about you of course and wouldn't even want to see me down there. If he decides to do it I'll wire you – otherwise I'll come on the North Shore as planned.

It's twenty-six whole hours since I wrote you last and I still love you. Every time I say it I hate to because it's so inadequate. Two more days and I can express it in the only way that's even half satisfactory. Nevertheless I love you –

Betty

38. Milwaukee, Monday [February 20, 1933]

Dear Bob –

I'm writing just a note before I take my customary Monday afternoon nap. I sincerely hope that your cold is better and that you're eating enough. If you don't stop getting sick nothing can prevent me from becoming as solicitous as your mother. Even though you are nice to take care of I prefer you well.

It seems to me that it would be a good idea to talk to Miss Bennett even if they aren't hiring anyone now.[73] We don't want to miss a chance. You must deal sternly with me about this job business. I'm full of ambition when I'm away from you but when I get to Chicago it seems absurd to do anything but be with you every minute of our brief weekends. It's been swell to drift for the last few weeks but the time has come to put a stop to it, I think. Have you heard any more about the corporation, by the way? I mean Business Equipment Bargains, Inc. or whatever it is?

I love you quite a bit more than I ever did – perhaps because I was somewhat unkind to you last evening. I'll never get that kind of an illness again. I'm irritable enough on occasion without that.

Love, Betty

---

72 Betty had excellent grades as a college student and was inducted into Phi Beta Kappa, the academic honor society, in her junior year.

73 See Letter 32, second paragraph.

39. Chicago, [Monday] Feb. 20, 1933 [the departure and arrival postmarks seem to indicate that it was sent Special Delivery, though the stamp is missing]

Dear Betty,

First I want to apologize to you for being so rude when you felt so sick at the dinner table last night. I shudder when I think how close I came to precipitating a genuine quarrel. I've always said that we ought to get a fight out of our systems but now I've come close enough to thoroughly dread such an event.

I suppose it was a disappointing week-end for you, due to the cold and ring trouble but let me say now, in connection with the ring, that what it costs is nobody's business but yours and mine. I didn't dare point that out last night, your mental and physical state being what it was, but I mention it now because my feeling on that point is rather acute.

Having gotten rid of that last bit of nastiness I can tell you how much I appreciate you. I have decided that it is rather silly and unfair of me to expect you to find a job in Chicago as a condition precedent to our marriage and I am making an earnest effort to get the law business in such shape as to keep us both although you will still be faced with the problem of spending your days somewhere outside the basement and it may mean a longer wait. However, I can see light ahead. I settled a case for the Bissell-Weiart Piano Co. today in a rather satisfactory matter and believe it will mean more work from them, which is the sort of client I need, even though they aren't doing very well at present, as who is?

Your Thursday letter just reached me today, as did the New Yorker. Fifteen cents out the window!

I don't understand at all why you love me unless you have some instinctive feeling that tells you I love you in spite of my clumsy and often harsh treatment of you. There is no reason why you should take my love for granted but I value more than I can say your willingness to rely on it in the face of very slight tangible evidence.

Bob

40. Milwaukee, Tuesday [February 21, 1933]

Dear Bob,

I think we're both making a mountain out of a molehill as far as last weekend's events are concerned. Don't you know that I understand you well enough not to be hurt by chance remarks you make, especially those when other people are around? There was nothing you said at dinner that wounded me in the least. I meant to tell you that I was amused at Stewart's and Nell's concern when I knew so much better than they what you meant.

The things that hurt a little you never realized and I forgave you for them two seconds later. Communication between two human beings, even two in love, is inevitably imperfect and I know that my errors are as unconscious and more frequent than yours.

I am glad you told me that one, though it hurt like hell at first to have you tell me - only because I feel such chagrin at having wounded you so thoughtlessly. I find it hard to forgive myself, but will you try to forget it and may I, too?

In spite of all this really unnecessary hashing by correspondence we have done, it was a pretty swell weekend, wasn't it? I got a positive thrill out of taking care of you the little I did, so you need never worry on my account about being sick.

I must mention that you're a fool - a nice one - but such a damn fool! You surround me with your thoughtfulness and love week after week and then write that I have "slight tangible evidence of it." I only hope to be considerate and responsible enough to give you the perfect satisfaction in my love that I have in yours.

It was smart of you to send the ad by Special Delivery. It sounds very promising and I answered with great dispatch in my most convincing manner.

I am delighted to hear of your successful settlement of the case and the possibilities it holds. There's no question of selfishness as far as our financial affairs are concerned, only a necessity for consistent cooperation. Both of us have to work hard on it, and which one of us reaches the minimum goal first is unimportant. One of us must - that's all.

I hope your New Yorker will arrive before Monday after this. I know that you will find it hard to save that fifteen cents if it doesn't.

Let's not take ourselves quite so earnestly in small matters after this. After all, there's quite a lot of fun in being in love --

Betty

41. Milwaukee, [Thursday, February 23, 1933; sent Special Delivery]

Dear Bob -

I hope this letter reaches you before Monday, for I intend to come to Chicago before that. I confidently expect to be able to take the twelve o'clock train which arrives at Grand Avenue at 1:53. I also confidently expect to receive a disconcerting telegram saying I am arriving at some other time! If I do change my mind I'll wire you, of course.

This can't be a very exciting letter because people keep coming in and I'm too self-conscious to be very personal.[74] I have missed you and thought of you constantly and I love you.

Betty

42. Chicago, [Thursday] Feb. 23, 1933 [sent Special Delivery]

Dear Betty,

Your letter was reassuring and comforting. I feel quite childish. The ring incident appears now as rather amusing inasmuch as Mr. Magnuson [*sic*] has placed the ring in his window with a fifteen dollar price tag on it. It seemed like a sacrilege at first and I was tempted to go in and finish buying it myself. I am afraid that I have given it a sentimental value in spite of my disapproval of the design and if you feel you want it I'll get it out of the window.

Stewart interrupted this letter by dropping in with some Haliver oil, free of charge. It should put me in great shape for the week-end.

Your Special Delivery letter just arrived in spite of having thirteen cents in stamps but it's just as well to have one of us unsuperstitious. I'll be at Grand Ave. at one fifty three Saturday and I hope your train will not keep me waiting again. I'm so crazy to see you that a delay at the station will kill me. Why it is that I can't become accustomed to the weekly four or five days separation is

---

[74] The letter is composed on Milwaukee Vocational School letterhead (see Illustration No. 21).

beyond me. Apparently love simply can't be organized on any rational basis. If only the first fire would wear off instead of becoming constantly more intense.

I love you is a common-place phrase and yet what more is there to say. I suppose I could put a row of x's or with some imagination, phrase the sentiment in lovely and fancy words innumerable times without repeating myself. But, on the whole, I'm suspicious of literary love. Look at Bernard Shaw and Ellen Terry.[75] At any rate you're in no danger from a verbal amorous assault. I want to do that physically and promptly – so help me.

Bob

43. Milwaukee, Monday [February 27, 1933]

Dear Bob –

I was disappointed when I realized that I had left the books behind again. I do feel that there's a certain progress in getting them as far as the Carsons and if we both strive earnestly enough I may get them here in another month or so.

I got a letter today from the accountant in Madison who has decided that I paid my sorority bill after all. Just another proof that it doesn't pay to worry. I am greatly relieved to have convinced him so easily.

I also received a letter from Mother who is apparently spending all her time worrying about us. It at least gives her a change in subject matter and is probably very good for her. I feel more than ever that I should go home, hard as it is. I tried to cheer her by remarking in a letter that she was nearer now to having the grandchildren she has wanted than ever before. She says that in her present state of health she fears having grandchildren would be too much for her. It's a little cruel to laugh at one's mother but just between ourselves that's too good a statement to refrain from mentioning, I think. It certainly puts the issue squarely up to us when Mother doesn't feel able to bear any grandchildren.

You were never quite so nice as you were last weekend. How you can improve on perfection so consistently I can't understand. If I could give you some slight idea of what you mean to me and how deeply I love you it would

---

75 *Ellen Terry and Bernard Shaw, An Intimate Correspondence*, edited by Miss Christopher St. John with a preface by Bernard Shaw, was first published by G. P. Putnam's Sons, New York, on October 2, 1931. The relationship between the famous playwright Shaw and well-known actress Terry was one of mutual admiration, but they only met in person once.

relieve me somewhat when I'm away from you. If I could, however, express all my feeling it wouldn't be love. You'll have to take a great deal of it for granted. Use all your imagination, though, to try to understand what you mean to me.

I love you,

Betty

44. Chicago, [Wednesday] Mar. 1, 1933

Dear Betty,

Here it is another month and practically nothing accomplished. The total "take" for the law business last month was only a hundred and twenty dollars and I am afraid I have been over-sanguine about its ability to produce a steady income. I still feel that I can make it go if general business conditions will only stop regressing (your word, I believe) but the present problem is how to succeed while the world around you is failing. Needless to say that problem is being solved everyday but it looks as though I shall have to use a little more ingenuity than heretofore, to be one of the solvers.

It is encouraging to learn that your mother has no more serious worries than grandchildren. Where would she be if she had you to worry about, as I have? That is I should worry about you but before I can get started you tell me again that you love me and I merely relax and congratulate myself on being the most successful man of our time. However, I do realize that having you married to me instead of merely in love with me, would make the success more evident and secure so I am rudely brought back to the measure of pecuniary rewards by the realization that I've got to succeed in making a living to marry you.

Personally, I should think you would be rather sick of hearing me continue to protest that I love you when I do so little about it. I can't understand myself, how I can love you so much and want to marry you more than anything else in the world and yet not do it. To think that such comparatively unimportant items as dollars and cents are holding me back seems incredible. It is incredible! I must really give the dollars and cents some serious attention and your visit to your mother gives me thirteen days for nothing else. Pay no attention if you don't hear from me. I shall be busy piling up a fortune.

Bob

45. Milwaukee, Wednesday [March 1, 1933]

Dear Bob -

I've been trying to fill my days with small affairs so that I won't miss you so much. I was so successful yesterday that I didn't have time to write you which is not what I intend. I had dinner with Margaret and then went to see Wheeler and Woolsey much against my will because she felt silly.[76] If she was trying to get over it she succeeded for both of us.

Tonight I am going to a guidance meeting[77] at a factory in West Allis. I do so wish you were here so that we could enjoy it together.

I have found out why I pay only one income tax and you ought to know, too, without my telling you. It all came back to me as soon as it was mentioned. No unit of government can tax income arising from another unit because the power to destroy is inherent in the power to tax and the integrity of the various units is thus protected. Since I am on the public payroll I pay no federal, but I do pay the state tax. The Wisconsin income tax system has several unique and very interesting features which I can explain if you wish. This is your lesson for today, however, and I don't want to give you more than you can absorb at one time.

My last letter was rather incoherent, I believe, because I was very sleepy, but it may have been better than this. Which do you prefer - sleepy, incoherent letters, or alert, didactic ones?

I have changed my mind completely about telling the administration of my marriage plans. Everyone for himself is my motto. The lesson in this, which I hope you won't learn too soon, is that you needn't take my problems seriously for I never think the same thing twice about them myself. If I didn't have problems I'd create them, though, for you're such a sympathetic listener. In other words, I love you, which is at once the source and solution of all problems for me, and the only thing of slightest importance I am thinking or writing.

Betty

[written up the left side of the last page]: P.S. This is absolutely the last of the envelopes I have been using up on you so you may look forward to matched

---

[76] Bert Wheeler and Robert Woolsey were a popular comic duo who made very successful films for RKO Studios from 1929–37.

[77] As Betty was a receptionist for a group of counselors at the Milwaukee Vocational School, this was probably a meeting related to her job there.

stationery from now on. If I find you haven't been taking your Haliver oil, you know what I'll do to you.

46. Chicago, [Thursday] Mar. 2, 1933

Dear Betty,

Your ultra smart letter has placed me in an unfortunate position. You have very neatly called my attention to a point of law that I completely overlooked and as I gaze at the row of books constituting my home law library I can't find one that deals with taxation.

However, admitting the correctness of your conclusion, my guess is that your reasoning is lousy. Needless to say the federal government taxes numerous articles and incomes which it has no intention of destroying. The reason it doesn't tax your income from the State of Wisconsin is that it feels bound to recognize the political sovereignty of that state and its right to carry on its internal political functions without interference from the federal government in the form of tax levies on salaries paid to its (the state's) employees. As the functions of the Milwaukee Vocational School are not governmental in character I have no doubt that a strict application of the theory would result in the federal taxation of your salary but the law is giving you a break by declining to distinguish between research counselors and persons usefully employed in administrative political units, as long as you all receive your compensation from the state. If you don't shut-up I intend to agitate for special legislation for federal surtaxes on all vocational school employees, scaled according to the size of school involved with the employees of the largest school, of course, paying the largest tax.

I am afraid that your failure to tell Mr. Cooley about your "marriage plans" was not due to a change of mind but simply because you haven't yet any (marriage plans - not mind). If you haven't I can't blame you but please keep marriage in mind because I love you and am at the same time somewhat conventional.

Bob

47. Milwaukee, Friday [March 3, 1933; sent Special Delivery]

Dear Bob -

My last letter seems to have really gotten you. I didn't really mean it to sound so smart but I now know one of your sensitive points and all knowledge I gain about you is useful. I think there were some weak points in my explanation, but not the ones you mention, and there were also logical flaws in your answer. I shall look into the matter and report in full at a later date.

I'm glad that you still love me, and also glad that you didn't leave the letter as reading that I had no mind, for I should have concluded you were really angry.

While I have no fault to find with this one, I should like to mention that the letter just previous was swell. It was characteristic of you to an unusual degree, which is enough to make me like anything. You have your own way of saying nice things which gives me quite a thrill sometimes.

I have just experienced an exciting day. I can recommend a bank holiday, that is, an unexpected one, as a general tonic for the nervous system as well as an interesting study in human psychology.

The details would be boring but the general outline is as follows. Our pay checks were released yesterday late in the afternoon, to my great relief, for the story has been for some weeks that we were not to be paid for four months.[78] The bank holiday this morning found me with ten dollars in cash which was much more than most people had. Late this morning it was found that the city treasurer, in spite of telephone statements to the contrary, was cashing our checks, so we rushed down in relays and all our office cashed their full salary checks. The result is that I have about one hundred dollars in one of the banks, the largest balance I have ever had at the end of a month, and about one hundred and forty-five dollars in my purse, which I don't know what the hell to do with. I think I shall put it in someone's safety deposit box. They are to be accessible, of course.[79]

---

78 The first page of *The Milwaukee Journal* for Thursday, March 2, 1933, has an article titled "City Is Paying Salaries; Debt Rule Revised" with the subtitle "Total of $1,000,000 Is Released for Public Employes [sic] Under New Deal on Cash Reserve." The first paragraph reads: "After a conference between city officials and the public debt commission, City Treasurer J. W. Murdoch at 1 p.m. Thursday released $1,000,000 from his tax collections to meet the February payroll of school employes and the payroll of city employes for the last half of February. Payment of the city employes began Thursday afternoon, a day late. The school employes will be paid on their regular payday next week."

79 *The Milwaukee Journal* for Friday, March 3, 1933, has a headline: "14-Day Suspension Ordered by State" with the subtitle "Milwaukee Leaders Confer on Ways to Carry on Business; Patrons Admitted to Safety Box Vaults on Showing Keys; Few Banks Here Decline to Comply with Closing Edict." The article says that the moratorium "was effective Friday morning and extends through Mar. 16," though it also mentions plans to open the banks in three to four days, and for the banks to permit

I don't know why I told you all this, for it doesn't give you any idea of the emotions we really went through, and sounds like a bold recital of how much money I have.

I don't know whether I'm lucky or unlucky in having marriage plans. That is the real cause of my having a balance in the bank.

All this is unimport[ant], however, and I really shouldn't have brought it up. I love you and you for some mysterious reason love me. Those are the two stable facts in my existence. Nothing that I can think of will shake those.

It hurts me that our marriage seems to depend on your exerting superhuman efforts to earn more money. I am enormously proud of your success thus far and I think you should be. Your achievement in establishing the practice you have and in gaining the independence you have is so much greater than its apparent measure in dollars and cents. If either of us has failed so far it is I.

I received a letter from Mr. Pugh. He says he is willing to talk to me if I can arrange to do so some Saturday morning though their plans have not progressed much farther. I am a little suspicious of him and his organization. He seems somewhat illiterate for a representative of a publishing house.

Speaking of publishing houses, one possible lead we have never investigated is the McGraw-Hill Co. They not only publish statistical magazines but are also interested in guidance texts. If we could find any contact there I'd like to find out about them.

I shall try to get a Saturday off soon and really accomplish something in the way of job hunting, though as Stewart so astutely remarked, other things are more fun.

I do love you so much, even though you are a problem, and though you don't know as much as you should about taxation.

Betty

---

deposits as well as allow some withdrawals on old accounts. It also names some Milwaukee banks that remained open, and others that "remained open to cash checks drawn on their own new deposits and transact business on old deposits under limitations." An editorial on the same day titled "Take It Easy, We're All in It" talked about the necessity for the Wisconsin banks to close after the many closings in other states, and that it was preferable to close rather than allow a "run" on all the banks. It said that the holiday "is first and foremost a plan to treat all alike" and called for everyone to share the burden.

48. Chicago, [Friday] Mar. 3, 1933 [sent Special Delivery]

Dear Betty,

I suppose that the Wisconsin moratorium has made you rather shy of cash. There were runs on all the banks here today, which will probably continue tomorrow. I'll be god damned if I'll join the hysterical mob and draw out money this week-end but when the panic calms down next week I will have to withdraw some cash for my own purposes and will get hold of some to send you at the same time.[80]

In the meantime, wire me collect at the office tomorrow, Mar. 4, if you are going to be pinched over the week-end and I'll send you some cash in a special to Madison to reach you Sunday.

This is a very instructive and mildly entertaining financial period that we find ourselves in and if we pull through it our grandchildren will have to listen to some tall tales. Remember to take it easy and don't let silly little trifles like bank suspensions crowd you. I'm just beginning to appreciate the tremendous advantage of being in love with you. I can't worry about money matters because they are so comparatively unimportant.

Bob

---

80 While the *Chicago Daily Tribune* of Friday, March 3, 1933, has an article about the governor of Illinois deciding there would be no moratorium on banks in the state, the Saturday, March 4, paper has a front page headline "3-Day Bank Holiday Here" with a subtitle "Illinois and N.Y. Agree on a Brief Moratorium." Part of the confusion in the different states resulted from the fact that while Franklin Delano Roosevelt had been elected to replace Herbert Hoover as president of the United States in November 1932, Hoover was still president until Roosevelt's inauguration on March 4, 1933. "The ratification of the Twentieth Amendment to the Constitution in February 1933 moved the start of the presidential term to January 20 of the year following the election, but the amendment would take effect only in 1937. Roosevelt's inaugural thus fell under the old rules and would not take place until March 4.... In the agonizing interval between Roosevelt's election in November 1932 and his inauguration in March 1933, the American banking system shut down completely. The global economy slid even deeper into the trough of the Depression" (David M. Kennedy, *Freedom From Fear, The American People in Depression and War, 1929–1945* [New York, Oxford: Oxford UP, 1999], 104). Kennedy indicates further that both Hoover and Roosevelt were doing a political dance in the situation, with Hoover wanting to vindicate his own record, and Roosevelt perhaps holding out so that the rescue operation could be attributed to him alone. Meanwhile, the American people were in a state of panic and anxiously awaiting deliverance from this crisis situation (Ibid., 105–112). The author gives further details about the panic during the banking crisis, and Roosevelt's resolution of it, in the beginning of his Chapter 5, "The Hundred Days" (Ibid., 131–139).

49. Milwaukee, Saturday [March 4, 1933; sent Special Delivery]

Dear Bob –

Your very thoughtful letter reached me this morning. You will learn from my letter that I am very well fixed for cash, as I am afraid you are not. If you or Stewart need money wire me in Madison – 114 N. Orchard – care of Mrs. Wm R Lloyd. I can send about ten dollars from there, and any sum up to eighty dollars on Monday morning, though I probably ought to keep about twenty of that.

I can't help being amazed at the similarity of your reactions to mine. I, too, refused to participate in a bank run. All during this situation I have marveled at how little it meant to me in comparison to the fact that you love me. I'm glad we're the same kind of damn fools.

Please let me help you and Stewart if I can.

Betty

50. Milwaukee, Monday [March 6, 1933]

Dear Bob,

I lay in bed Sunday morning waiting for your telegram and as usual you didn't fail me. Why can't I be as nice to you as you are to me?

I spent a very pleasant quiet weekend and I am very glad I went home. It relieves my mind and eases my conscience and now I 'm free again to think of nothing but you. I eased Mother's mind of her present worries about us, though I know she will find some new ones before I see her again. She was very nice, though, and she hopes that we can get married soon.

I realized more than ever what you have done for me. When Mother has been in this disturbed state of mind before I have always found myself succumbing to her attitude of gloom and defeat to the extent that I was unable to help her even temporarily. With you in my thoughts I can't be depressed and I really think she felt much better when I left. It's just a small indication of the emotional strength and balance your love gives me.

I got up at dawn this morning to drive back with my erratic friend Danny who could not tear himself away from his girl to take me home last night. I am determined to get him to Chicago some time and do the same for him. He has the tactical advantage of being the driver and car owner so the idea is rather hard to work out.

It's almost worth staying away from you for a weekend to feel the added happiness it will be to see you again. Last week was immeasurably long but this one will be a minute.

I am forced to close to go to a Sigma Kappa[81] meeting which I have passed up for two months.

I love you more each minute of my life. I held myself so in check last week that I don't see how I can bear it much longer. Just four days and I'll see you and touch you -

I love you -

Betty

51. Milwaukee, Tuesday [March 7, 1933]

Dear Bob,

I called you last night when I came home but you didn't answer. I was so excited to find you had called and so let down when I couldn't talk to you. We're very unlucky about telephone calls. That is the first Monday I've been out for months. I'd like to call you tonight but I'm entertaining my bridge club and I think I'd better not be rude about it, even if I do like you better.

I was wrong about this week. It's one of the longest ones already that I've ever spent.

It seems so unnecessary to tell you again - but I do love you.

Betty

52. Chicago, [Wednesday] Mar. 8, 1933

Dear Betty,

Monday night was really tragic. I was in the tub with the water running when you called and shut it off in time to hear the last ring, at the sound of which I dashed to the phone, leaving pools of water in my wake, and grasped the receiver just late enough to get nothing but the familiar dial tone. I felt certain it was your call, knowing your extravagant habit of returning my call whether I ask you to or not, so I called the long distance operator to ask about calls from Milwaukee but got no satisfaction from her. Then I cursed the telephone

---

81 Sigma Kappa was the sorority Betty joined at the University of Wisconsin.

company, our noisy plumbing and what I have now identified as your Sigma Kappa meeting, impartially and went to bed. This illustrates the futility of scientific planning as you agree that the call was perfectly timed for normal conditions. I suppose the perfect sequel would be a call from you tonight while I am at the Golden Gloves tournament. All this about the telephone call shows you how people write those ten page letters to one another daily, from which you have been spared so far.

I trust that your bridge club was successfully entertained last night, probably with some bridge such as it had never seen before. You are beginning to remind me of a social butterfly, apparently just a party girl.

Seriously, what you do isn't the slightest concern of mine so long as you feel the way you say you do, except what you do with, to and for me. You've worked me up to such a pitch now that I need a nice, prosaic letter to calm me down - but don't write it. I can't make decent love to you by mail and I am sick of repeating those silly words "I love you" but I never get tired of seeing them in your handwriting.

I don't love you any more. That is apparent to me. No such banal word can describe my present feeling nor does it do any good to recite the cold facts that you are my sole reason for existence and more a part of my life than I am myself as a description of our relationship. None of it is objective enough for words, or any other medium of expression, for that matter. Even if I were an artist I couldn't paint it for you. All I can do is conventionalize and sentimentalize it with the statement I love you - a mere half-truth. Not even a half-truth, in fact. Just a mere suggestion of a feeling or state or condition that has nothing to do with truth or falsity but which is the only, the ultimate reality of my being. All I can hope from those three words is that you are able to reconstruct from them the feeling that I can only feel but dully attempt to express by them, by means of your own identical feeling, which I know exists, not because you've tried to convey the knowledge to me with those same words but because I - well, I suppose because I love you. Wow!

Bob

53. Milwaukee, Wednesday [March 8, 1933]

Dear Bob -

I know that I could find a great deal to talk to you about if you were here, but I can't think of anything to write you about. The underlying reason for that is that I'm very tired.

I shall try to meet you at one fifty-three Saturday at Grand Avenue, unless you have another plan. I may have to come an hour later but I'll let you know in that case. I think Pat will let me leave early.

I wish that I could write you a swell letter tonight but the mind is dull. I still love you, however, and I'm counting the hours until I see you.

Betty

54. Milwaukee, Monday [March 13, 1933]

Dear Bob -

I can't have a successful nap while I'm thinking how much I love you so I might as well write you.

I can't decide yet whether it was selfish and wrong of me to hurt you and disturb you as I did Saturday night but you dissolved my strange feelings so completely that the result of it will make us both happier, I think. Not only did you help me, but you let me understand some things which should enable me [to] help you more in the future to avoid misunderstanding my reactions. I hope that you will tell me the things that worry or disturb you without any reserve for fear of hurting me. It's the only way I can learn to be all to you that I want to be. I do love you so completely, though sometimes it's even harder for me to tell you about it when I'm with you than to express it satisfactorily in writing.

This was to be quite a long letter but I find I have to leave now. I have told you the important part and if I have expressed myself adequately you know most of what I'm thinking.

I love you so much now that I don't see how it can grow at all from now on, but if the past is an indication it will.

Betty

55. Chicago, [Tuesday] Mar. 14, 1933

Dear Betty,

Please don't scold yourself about Saturday night. I have felt so sure and confident of your love for me that it was just as well to make me stop and think - not take so much for granted. But when you keep reiterating your feeling for me in your physical behaviour and letters I can scarcely help being convinced. The potential tragedy in the situation, if any, lies in my being so completely yours and permanently built around you that I simply couldn't comprehend your ceasing to love me regardless of what you might tell me.

I stopped in at Mr. Magnussen's today and saw a page full of sketches he has made for rings that intrigued me greatly. I told him we would be in to see him Saturday, when he says he will have some more sketches and some of them partly worked out in the actual metal so that we won't delude ourselves so completely again. It seems to me that getting you a satisfactory ring is more important than anything else right now because we've got to have that for our marriage no matter what happens.

Last night I bowled with the Mayer, Meyer employees[82] and had one game of 97. Don't ask me about the others, though. You will have to regain your early form to beat me.

From your letter I judge that the "curse" finally caught up to you in the midst of it and you are apparently not going to set a new American record for female periods or have a baby. Anyway you ought to be at your peak for the coming week-end - if it ever gets here. If I take in a fee maybe we can go dancing - just to ease your mother's mind. The next time you see her remind her that I love you.

Bob

56. Milwaukee, Tuesday [March 14, 1933]

Dear Bob -

The next time you see Bess Cunningham be sure to thank her for the picture of you she gave me. It's an ever-growing delight to me. Your expression of mingled emotion is such that even if the baby were cut off, one could tell that you were undergoing some strange experience. You'd better practice up on that stuff if you ever expect to be President. Even a Justice of the Supreme Court may

---

82 Mayer, Meyer, Austrian, and Platt was the law firm where Bob worked from 1930-32.

have to hold babies - you can't tell—and as husband of the secretary of labor you'd have to make a profession of it.

Enough of that. But speaking of babies reminds me that I mean to bring the family album back from Madison so that I could show you what a brat I was. Would you like to see it? Stewart and Gordon were really cute, so there may be some hope for our children, especially as you were so sweet. When you finish this letter please send it to Bernarr McFadden for the next issue of "Babies—Just Babies."[83]

Mary and Porter have discovered a swell walk that we can take the next time you come to Milwaukee. It goes along the lake shore.

You're still my candidate for the perfect husband. I don't see how I can lose with you. If after ten years or so I no longer want to rush into your arms the moment we're alone I'll still be interested by you and admire you. Perhaps that picture doesn't please you as much as it does me. Nevertheless as much as I love you physically and as much as I value that love, the thing that makes me sure I'm right is that I can't imagine your ever boring me or losing place in my esteem. But right now I simply love you in all ninety-nine ways -

Betty

57. Milwaukee, Wednesday [March 15, 1933]

Dear Bob -

It's always something - Now the stationery has given out. This large blank sheet gives me pause, to use a phrase of yours which always amuses me, though I doubt that I've used it correctly.

I can't imagine what I said to give you the idea that I had the "curse". I haven't, which amuses me so that I have ceased to worry about it and I feel perfectly normal again. I don't regard this as an appropriate subject in correspondence, but since you brought it up I'll add that I was amused to read the remark you referred to in "Young Woman of 1914". You realize of course that

---

83 A magazine published by Bernarr McFadden's company, edited by Mrs. Franklin D. Roosevelt until May of 1933, when she had to stop doing so, due to "the 'onerous character of her duties at the White House' and the difficulty of finding time for her magazine duties" (*Chicago Daily Tribune*, May 5, 1933, p. 2, column with headline "Mrs. Roosevelt Quits 'Babies, Just Babies'; Magazine to Stop").

the first few months of love which she mentions refer to an entirely different situation from the one we find ourselves in.[84]

Your letters do something very special for me. When I come in the door at night I say to myself, "I probably won't get a letter tonight and it doesn't matter a bit", and then when I see it all the rational attitude I've created leaves instantly. It's so silly but it's true. And you have such peculiarly nice ways of saying "I love you."

You're quite right to be confident of my love. Don't ever stop being so. I want you more than ever. Loving you is the only thing which gives my life any significance. It's incredible to think of existing without you.

I have a feeling that this next weekend is going to be particularly exciting because I want to see you so badly. You don't need to take me dancing, either, though I can't seem to convince you of that. It's so typically nice of you to take that to heart as you did, but why can't you believe that I want to see you without crowds as much as I think you do me? You can't buy my love, sir. I'm giving it to you – more than I can ever tell you –

Betty

[written up left side of page]: P.S. I'll plan to arrive at 1:53, Grand Avenue, again, though I don't know how to manage it. I guess Pat will let me out early, though. I'm glad to hear about the rings. We should be able to solve that problem.

No date [from Gary, Indiana]

[85]My dear boy – Are you sure you have a not a very frayed, collared blue shirt which David[86] is missing and wants to have ________ [?] as he is very limited in shirts. Please look and send back clean or otherwise.

---

84 The *Chicago Daily Tribune* of Friday, December 2, 1932 (p. 23) has a review of *Young Woman of 1914* by Arnold Zweig, due to be published the following day by Viking Press. It is a love story set in Potsdam at the beginning of World War I. The review says: "Though there are many older characters in the book, who are, like the younger ones, vastly affected by the war, both emotionally and spiritually, the emphasis is laid upon the emergence of a new youth, in particular a new womanhood." It concludes: "'Young Woman of 1914' is an impressive book, memorable for many reasons, not the least of which is its creation of a beautiful idyl of love, a love struggling against obstacles and seeking expression." Zweig (1887–1968) was a German Jewish writer, an active pacifist, a Zionist, and later a socialist who lived in the German Democratic Republic after 1948 until his death. He is best known for his World War I tetralogy, of which *Young Woman of 1914* is one part.

Pesh[87] has a birthday April 1st & mine being March 22nd we usually celebrate together. As for me I would be glad to pass over the date but it all means so much to Pesh so we expect to do something a little different – We wonder if you and Betty would like to come out and have dinner with us probably on Sunday March 26th –

I will be in town April 1st, at a luncheon for Judge Barteline.

Perhaps you would like to come out here March 25th and spend the night.

Just let us know what plan will suit you.

Perhaps John & Hazel[88] can also come in March 26th. Nothing very fancy of course but just a get together. One of those family gatherings you know. Perhaps Betty would like to see a sample – I expect to be in town all day Monday March 20 – Club Board Meeting I have in morning. I hope to have better luck in reaching you by phone that day –

Expect daily to hear of the new arrival at Catherine's.[89]

With much love

Yours, Mother

---

85 This letter to Bob from his mother was filed with the courtship letters. There is no day or date on the letter and no envelope. It refers to an upcoming visit to Chicago on Monday, March 20, as well an invitation for Betty and Bob to spend the night on March 25, and have dinner with other family members on March 26, 1933. Betty refers to this visit in Letters No. 60, first paragraph, and No. 63, second paragraph.

86 David Samuel Wright was the fourth child of Frank Lloyd and Catherine Tobin Wright (b. September 26, 1895; d. November 1, 1997).

87 "Pesh" may refer to Ben Page, the man Bob's mother married in June 1930. See n.6.

88 See n. 68. John Lloyd Wright (b. John Kenneth Wright December 12, 1892; d. December 20, 1972) was the second child of Frank Lloyd and Catherine Tobin Wright. After a first marriage to Jeannette Winter in 1914, which ended in divorce in 1920, he married Hazel Lundin on October 27, 1921. They had two children, Elizabeth Lloyd Wright (b. July 26, 1923), and John Lloyd Wright, Jr. (b. February 23, 1925; d. January 30 1974).

89 Catherine Dorothy Wright was Bob's oldest sister, and his parents' third child (b. January 12, 1894; d. January 27, 1979). She married Kenneth Baxter on March 11, 1919. They had three children, only one of whom survived past childhood: James Stewart Baxter (b. January 24, 1920; d. June 2, 1920); Anne Baxter, the actress (b. May 7, 1923; d. December 12, 1985), and Richard Tobin Baxter (b. April 2, 1933; d. November 24, 1936). The reference must be to the imminent birth of Richard.

58. Milwaukee, [Monday March 20, 1933?][90]

Dear Bob -

My train got in at five this morning after battling the eighty miles foot by foot. There was no chance to sleep with all the goings-on. I was unhappy and lonesome and wished you were there so you could be unhappy, too. I'm surprised that I am as conscious as I am this morning. The thing that distressed me most was being forced to stay awake and miss you for five hours while you were happily oblivious of me.

Put me away in some obscure corner of your mind this week and don't neglect your law business. You know what I want to tell you and am completely unable to. How can two people feel as we do? I am reduced to saying I love you.

Betty

59. Chicago, [Tuesday] Mar. 21, '33

Dear Betty,

Here I am at home at 4:30 to answer your letter, because I'm going out to dinner—and no letter.[91] But on this, the first day of the fourth season of our acquaintance I feel impelled to write you anyway. You will, of course, have to promptly be at your worst and stay that way until fall to make good on your own forecast and I am looking forward to your spring worst with considerable interest, having had only a fleeting glimpse of your summer worst or am I thinking of summer sausage.

Just to punish you I'm not even going to tell you that I love you except that I want to marry you the worst way for better before you get worse.

Bob

---

[90] The postmark on the envelope is torn; only PM and the year 1933 can be read. The stationery and envelope have the Milwaukee Vocational School letterhead. The letter seems to fit in the context with the subsequent ones in the week of March 20, 1933.

[91] Bob doesn't get Betty's previous letter, No. 58, until Thursday. See his letter No. 62.

60. Milwaukee, Tuesday [March 21, 1933]

Dear Bob –

I'm sorry I'm so forgetful about stationery. You deserve nothing but the best.[92] It has occurred to me that if you are giving your mother a birthday present I should like to help you, unless you think that in my present anomalous position it would be bad taste. I feel that I owe her quite a lot. May I do it?

There is another matter that deserves our consideration, perhaps even more than the ring. How are we going to have our first quarrel? It seems to me we're getting farther away from it all the time, and I must rely on you to cooperate in this matter much better than you have in the past. I'm going to tell my mother that you know I love to fight but you never fight with me –

I've resolved not to tell you that I love you in this letter. The utter, sickening futility of that phrase is beginning to get me. The futility of trying to describe what this thing is that I feel is even greater, but what else have I to write you about? When I'm with you I find myself existing on a plane above that of ordinary living and quite unrelated to it. There is no longer myself nor yourself, but only that strange fusion of both in which we have no separate identities. I realize that I am getting beyond my depth, and perhaps beyond yours in that my expression of a concept that I really see is faulty, but it's such an amazing, miraculous phenomenon to me. And it's a foolishly satisfying thought to me also, that since there are no two people just like us, no other two could have exactly the experience that we do, even though we go through the eternal silly motions of the race –

Betty

61. Milwaukee, Wednesday [March 22, 1933]

Dear Bob –

You're nuts! In the first place I write you a letter every Monday, tired as I am, and keep right on writing far on into the week and you think you ought to wait until you hear from me! Think how excited I'd be if I ever got a letter on Tuesday-

Beside all that, you're nuts anyway. Sausages, indeed! I don't believe you love me. It's just fun for you, no doubt.

---

92 The letter is written on a coarser and plainer sheet than Betty usually uses.

I went to the Jones' for dinner tonight. Little sister is home from college and we had a nice little sing around the piano. Why don't you learn to play before we get married so that we can play and sing in the long evenings?

Incidentally where do you get this 4:30 stuff? You're supposed to be hewing to the line in my absence. It doesn't take you that long to write a one page letter.

Enough of reprimanding you. When I find you so miraculously without faults I have to invent some, just to keep you in your place.

I bought a nightgown today, a rather silly affair. Will that do for the present if I can't find a hat I like? At least I'm spending, and for your eventual pleasure, I hope, if not your immediate satisfaction.

I've missed you so this week. It seems so impossible that you really love me – as you won't say you do – when you're not here where I can see and hear and feel you. I can't help believing that this feeling of ours is just a beginning – that being with you all the time will make it more significant. And because I believe this I can wait, even though my longing to be with you is almost insupportable at times – Betty

[Written up the side of the page:] P.S. I'll try to make the same train though again I don't know how I'll do it. I love you –

62. Chicago, [Thursday] Mar. 23, 1933

Dear Betty,

The United States mails are unaccountable. I got your Monday's letter today, and Tuesday's yesterday. You must have had a terrible trip. I suppose we might have anticipated the electric trouble and gotten you a ticket on the Northwestern but I had no idea it was that serious. Anyway, you got there safely, although I'll confess that I went to sleep without worrying much about you, even though it took me about an hour to get home on the street-car.

It was very nice of you to think of a gift for Mother but I think we can solve that problem by taking down some flowers and don't feel that your position is anomalous insofar as my family are concerned because they have all been assured that we are going to get married.

But are we? Sometimes it seems as though we never will. We just drift along in hope without even approaching the goal.

We feel, of course, that our love is the only true reality with which we are confronted, but in disregarding the actualities of the world around us or rather regarding them as illusions, we can't hope to marry into them. I sometimes feel that my emotional state is absolutely incompatible with the problems of the business of getting married and yet marriage seems at the same time to be the only means of preserving and making permanent the emotional state.

The solution, obviously, is a balanced mind or at least emotional poise of some sort but how to achieve that is something else. It can't be done by total absence from each other and while I'm completely happy when we're together I can't help feeling the impermanence of that happiness even then. Whether marriage and a temporary life apart will help I don't know but I feel that before many more weeks pass it might be seriously considered.

Bob

63. Milwaukee, Monday [March 27, 1933]

Dear Bob –

I've thought of nothing all day but how nice it will be to have you here next weekend. I went to the Shorecrest for dinner tonight and I felt like running up to our headwaiter to tell him you were coming. I didn't – Milwaukee really seems like a place instead of a vague something or other that keeps me from you. I'm a damn fool, I know, to go on like this, but I'm so in love with you that anything I can somehow relate to you takes on a new significance. Some day I hope to regain my sanity with you but right now you'll have to be insane with me.

I enjoyed going to Gary with you – I'm sure I'm never going to have any family-in-law troubles. I like them all and I think your mother is an especially admirable person.

It's rather silly of me, but I felt a certain pride in being there in a recognized position as your intended, shall I say – The other time I felt as though I really were in an anomalous position because so much had been implied and so little said. I suppose it's just an urge to bind you to me in every possible way – Since I can't love you wholly right now, I want to be sure that everyone knows I have an important claim on you.

The Easter weekend will be three weeks from now, I am told. Start thinking about the Monday or Friday problem. I really think that some strenuous job hunting should be done on that day. We've got to find the answer soon, and I think that would be a very happy one.

I love you –

Betty

[Written up side]: P.S. I just got the curse – Tuesday morning – Will that shut you up?

26. Betty with some of the women in Bob's family, 1933. L. to r.: Bob's mother, Betty, Bob's sister Catherine, Bob's brother John's wife Hazel

27. Bob and Betty, 1933

64. Milwaukee, Wednesday [March 29, 1933]

Dear Bob –

Why didn't I get a letter from you today? It's raining and a letter would have helped the general situation quite a bit. I, however, didn't write you last night due to unforeseen circumstances, so perhaps I deserve it. And besides I never can decide whether I love you more when you write me or when you don't. It's about even.

The week is rounding out nicely. Last night I went out, tonight I'll read, tomorrow I play bridge and Friday I won't need anything to divert me – I'll be so excited about your coming. A futile life, isn't it? I'm rather annoyed at myself for not finding more interesting things to do without you. I'm afraid it indicates a lack somewhere. My only major worry about our marriage is that I may bore you after a time. I've always been afraid of that because I'm so sure that you won't bore me, and I want to be best, even in that. I used to have faith that I was year by year becoming a more interesting person, and that someday I should be something very special.

Don't let me become too dependent on you for ideas. What I expect you to do about it I can't tell. It's my problem. Nevertheless in my characteristic way I ask you to solve it, without meaning that you should. What I mean is that I love you and I'm not half the person I want to be so that I may feel I really deserve such a swell guy.

Betty

65. Chicago, [Wednesday] Mar. 29, 1933

Dear Betty,

I understand now why your Monday letters reach me on Wednesday. You hold them till Tuesday for a postscript but I suppose it was worth waiting another day to learn that I hadn't really been betrayed after all. You had better report to Edris or she will suspect me of betraying you. I appreciate your timing but still, when Saturday comes, there probably won't be any tangible proof of your alleged condition left and I may suspect you of fabricating your story to conceal your true condition unless you display an unusual amount of affection.

I played anagrams last night but failed to distinguish myself. All I could think of to take canapé was pancreas with pancake staring me in the face. Now that I think it over panacea would have been a nice way to do it too.

The law business has been disappointing for me this week as a client whom I billed for a two hundred dollar fee has all her money in one of the few banks that have failed to reopen here. She had heard about you and expressed the hope that she could pay me soon to help the marriage plans along but I was forced to confess that they weren't imminent.

Anyway I'll see you in Milwaukee Saturday and I trust that you have made a reservation for me at the Mills House and just because at the moment I can't think of any new and striking way of saying I love you don't think I don't.

Bob

66. Chicago, [Wednesday] Mar. 29, 1933

Dear Betty,

Edris called me today and said she and Bob would move the middle of next week, possibly to the south side, and suggested that perhaps you would want to come down this week-end to make use of the present space for the last time. It doesn't make any difference to me whether I go to Milwaukee this week or next and I shall call you on the phone tomorrow night (Friday) at about ten o'clock, to find out what you think about it. According to your letter you aren't doing anything tomorrow night anyway so you had better be home.

I bought a set of wooden anagrams today for you and we ought to give them a work-out over the week-end – maybe I bought them for myself.

Please stop telling me what a dull girl you are or someday I will turn on you and believe it. I keep searching you for deficiencies each time I see you and when I find one I notify you at once but I am afraid that you are willfully blinding yourself to mine, which will eventually result in an accumulation that may be too much for you when and if you ever get your eyes open. What I want from you is not blind faith but some critical, analytical love. How can I ever get you to make something out of me when you concentrate on yourself. Leave yourself alone and give me some attention. There, you see how selfish I really am, asking not merely for affection but alteration as well.

If you could only be made aware of the deadly self-satisfaction that seizes me when you make those extravagant declarations of feeling you would instantly retract them but I hope you never do. I don't tell you I love you do I. I tell you what's wrong with you in the vain hope that I can make myself believe that you're not really absolute perfection but someone I can reasonably hope to live with on even terms.

Bob

67. Milwaukee, Monday [April 3, 1933]

Dear Bob –

I have just read a few more chapters of Clarence Darrow's book.[93] The perfect simplicity of his style alone makes it worth reading. That sort of style has always seemed to me the greatest, and I suppose the hardest to achieve.

I hope that you are not more tired than I am today. This business of sleeping a lot is silly. I feel better than usual.

I have been wondering what your attitude is on my finding a job. You seemed a trifle annoyed when I mentioned it last night, though I don't attach undue importance to that. It still seems to me that I must make every reasonable effort in that direction: first because it isn't fair for you to bear the whole responsibility for achieving our marriage, and second because our present situation is so distressing. It must be so to you, since it is to me. I'm not afraid to face any of the numerous problems that will confront us after marriage. Those would be tangible in comparison to the false and unnatural ones which our present relationship creates. There seem to be no rules in this game, no accepted pattern of conduct, no way to tell whether we're doing right or wrong nor what the result will be. Essentially the basis for my worry is the fear of losing you, not by some direct blow, but by unconsciously and unmeaningfully injuring the relationship. I have come a long way from my original point that I believe I ought to try harder to find a job. I do want to know whether you feel that you ought to do it all yourself, which is wrong, whether you too are anxious for me to find one, or whether you're just so fatigued by the situation that you don't give a damn.

This is rather a solemn letter. Keeping a combined sense of humor is perhaps the best answer. You can help me achieve that. If we lose it now we may never regain it and I am told that marriage requires a lot of it.

---

93 Clarence Darrow published *The Story of My Life* in 1932 (New York, London: C. Scribner's Sons), and it was on the Best Seller List for Nonfiction in the *Chicago Daily Tribune* of March 5, 1932. Darrow (1857–1938), who moved to Chicago in 1887, had a career full of controversy as a criminal defense lawyer and a strong opponent of the death penalty. His most well-known cases were as the defense attorney for the teenage sons of two wealthy Chicago families, Leopold and Loeb, accused of murdering and kidnapping another teenager in 1924, and as the attorney who defended the teacher John Scopes in 1925 in a trial centering on the teaching of evolution in public schools. In 1932, after his retirement, he took on another extremely controversial case as the defense attorney for white men accused of murdering a Hawaiian man. The latter was one of a group of men who had been charged, probably falsely, with the rape of a white woman.

I love you very deeply and I want above all to do the correct things to make you happy.

Betty

68. Chicago, [Tuesday] April 4, 1933

Dear Betty,

Words! Words! Words! And such words! Words like "unmeaningfully"! Phrases like "the correct things to make you happy"! What rhetoric! What passion!

So you want to know whether I think you should look for a job or whether I should look for a job for you or whether I care, do you? Well pay attention to this. I think you should get married. If you can support the man you marry so much the better but don't wait for that or you may never marry. That's what I did.

Seriously, I think your renewed interest in job hunting is commendable and I can't see that an earnest effort in that direction would do any harm but I am afraid that you may be putting the cart before the horse. It seems to me that a job here should be incidental to your marriage [rather] than the basis for it. I am still clinging, though somewhat desperately, to the May 1 deadline for the marriage but have more or less given up that date for the establishment of a home with you, except on week-ends. I don't feel that you can afford to leave the School much before June 1 or that I can properly propose to receive you as a permanent guest much before that time. However, I do feel as you do, that the present situation is rapidly becoming intolerable, which puts us in complete accord.

The thing to remember is that love is the only proper subject of correspondence between lovers worthy of the name. And yet you want to exchange affidavits. Some day I am going to find my book "How to Write Letters" and send you number 51, from a young man offering himself in marriage to the lady of his choice. Then, and only then, will you appreciate my abandoned expression of tender sentiments, come to admire the chaste simplicity of my "Elizabeth, I love you" and care for me as you do Clarence Darrow. In the meantime I want to see you, preferably in a marriage bed with me, so badly that it hurts to merely write you.

Bob

69. Milwaukee, Tuesday [April 4, 1933]

Dear Bob –

I feel so sorry for you the day after I write you a morbid letter like my last. It relieves my petty worries but it's rather a selfish way of doing so. You may be assured that I'm quite contented with my lot today. I can't think of anyone I'd want to be except the girl you are in love with.

In reply to your letter of last week I may say that there is something in your statement that I concentrate on myself too much and on you too little. As far as remolding your character is concerned I'm afraid I can't do much now. In my most sober and unemotional moments I find any criticism I can make of you so superficial, and unimportant that it would be absurd to mention it. Essentially you are the sort of person I admire and want to be with. I want to help you in every possible way but constructive criticism is impossible for me in my present state of mind. I'm really trying to be serious about this. I think you're human, and I expect [to] live with you on fairly even terms in spite of my imperfections. You happen to fulfill my specifications. How can I try to change you?

I hope you can find Mr. Magnussen this week without too much trouble. That is a strange complication. Perhaps he moved to get away from our annoying indecisions.

I have been trying to call you this evening, and if I don't get you, I shall have to write a second installment of this letter. Please come home right now. It will be so nice to talk to you.

I still love you,

Betty

[written up the side of the page:] P.S. You were at home. It's nice of you to keep early hours. It was swell to hear your voice and it will be even better to see you Saturday.

70. Milwaukee, Wednesday [April 5, 1933]

Dear Llewellyn –

I find your letter very confusing. I plead guilty to being rhetorical. However, in one paragraph you say that the only subject for correspondence between lovers is love, and imply that the only permissible expression of it is a chaste "I love you". That doesn't fill four pages, you know. What am I to do? Why do I "want to exchange affidavits"? I think I know what the word means, but the thought escapes me. If you continue to write such hasty illogical letters I shall begin to doubt your ability as a lawyer. Please try to organize them after this.

You once wrote me a perfect letter. I doubt if you will ever achieve such a one again, I know that I shall never, and I doubt if Clarence Darrow could. When I write my volume on how to write letters that will certainly be included. It was the one in which you first told me you love me. It erased the last doubt from my mind. Since I first loved you for your literary style I feel that I can criticize when I find you becoming slipshod.

Paul Muni is here this week in "Counsellor at Law".[94] I know that you have seen it, but if you think it worth seeing again with him I should like to take you Saturday night. You might give it your consideration. I think I can get tickets after you come. I suppose, however, that you will want to spend all your time drinking beer and getting red in the face.

I planned to have you get this letter tomorrow but it's raining so hard that you may never get it and what's more I may never get my dinner.

Who's putting the cart before the horse, you or me?

Betty

71. Chicago, [Wednesday] April 5, 1933

Dear Betty,

I called Mr. Pugh this morning and he is willing to see you a week from Saturday instead of this Saturday. He wants you to call him at about seven o'clock on the Friday night you arrive here to make an appointment for the following morning. He also said he could make you a better proposition than he did before if you are still interested – whatever that means. No doubt if you work up a fast enough sales talk he will insist on giving you an advance on your prospective royalties.

Apparently you felt that your business call excused you from writing a letter. It's about the only unsolicited phone call I can remember your giving me but as it wasn't to tell me you loved me it doesn't count. Remember, the period is

---

94 *The Milwaukee Journal* of Sunday April 2, 1933, announced a week's run of Elmer Rice's *Counsellor at Law* starring Paul Muni at the Davidson Theater in Milwaukee, with the original Broadway cast and production, which "even Chicago didn't see." The play is reviewed very favorably by Richard S. Davis in the same paper on Tuesday, April 4, 1933.

rapidly approaching when you are at your theoretical emotional peak. I am not at all sure that it will be safe for me to spend this week-end with you in Milwaukee but I am going to risk it.

But never mind. One of the things I love you for is your restraint not to mention your unconscious ability to make me forget mine. I love you for so many things that I know they can't all be illusory. You must have some of them, really, by the law of averages, and any one would be enough. What troubles me is that you may be literally too good to be true, in the sense of being true to me. It really isn't necessary for me to invent faults. Your perfection can easily be regarded as one and you see I have already made it the cause of a completely suppositious unfaithfulness.

Maybe I had better stick to the stock terms of endearment, sweetheart, or I shall find myself quarreling with you absolutely unassisted. Anyway, why don't you write me you dirty little bum?

Bob

72. Chicago, [Thursday] April 6, 1933

Dear Betty,

An affidavit is a written statement under oath - serious - get the thought? I'm afraid you don't like being kidded. Or are you kidding me? If you didn't enjoy Tuesday's letter what must you have thought of Wednesday's? I apologize for the unjust accusation about failing to write although I haven't yet understood your method of mailing that brings letters written on different days here at the same time.

It was very nice of you to offer to take me to see "Counsellor-at-law." I should like very much to see Muni play it but I will get the tickets. My only suggestion is that we might go in the afternoon if there is a marked difference in price and you have no other plans.

Edris has a little girl. It seems to have happened rather suddenly last night. I expect to be able to visit her at the hospital next week - Women's and Children's is the very appropriate name, if you want to send her a wire.

If I can fill this full of neighborhood gossip perhaps it will be the perfect letter. But the perfect letter for you and me is certainly not the readable letter. It is, I hope, the letter that best expresses the mood of the writer. The letter you called perfect was written when I loved you in a calm, almost calculating manner. I love you now with a mad feverishness that can only be expressed in extravagantly illogical, even ludicrous, phrases, when I write you. I give vent to the torture of our separation in a way that permits me to let off steam without emphasizing or increasing your share of it by means of soft sentiment. I only feel genuinely sentimental when I'm with you. If I wrote seriously about my feeling for you while away from you I would expose its desperate impotence which of course disappears when I have you near me and can really love you. Not really love you either but at least hold you in my arms and test your reality by actual although superficial contact.

All this sounds as though I loved you for your body which I don't give a damn for, in itself. I love you as a complete character, more for the quality of your thought and spirit than anything else but I can't make love, in the best sense of the word, to that on paper at a distance of ninety miles, or ninety feet, for that matter. I carry you as an ideal in my head and in my heart always but what has that to do with pen and ink. In a completely emotional situation pen and ink are worthless. They're worse – but why continue to prove the point. All that I can reasonably do is thank God that I'm going to be with you Saturday and shut up.

Bob

P.S. I am going to find Mr. Magnuson [*sic*] tomorrow, so help me!

Llewellyn

73. Milwaukee, Thursday [April 6, 1933]

Dear Bob –

I hope you are ashamed of yourself now that you have received the letter I sat up that night to finish. I really didn't intend to write you today – you certainly don't deserve it. But when you call me a dirty little bum, not to mention sweetheart, underlined to be sure I don't miss the sarcasm, a reply is called for. I think you're a louse yourself –

There is a certain flattery in your worries about my faithfulness and I suppose for my own security I ought to encourage them. I have always hoped I should fall in love with the kind of man who wouldn't have to be cajoled or fretted into loving me, and I think I have. I don't think I'm capable of playing a game even to keep you. I hope you'll always love me because you're sure of my love and not because you doubt it.

I had fun at the office today for the first time in months. Van and I had to make charts for a speech of Mr. Patterson's and I love to make charts. I was singing your song (and Ruth Etting's) "Sweet Daddy" and imagine my surprise when Van joined in with all the words and variations. Perhaps he is the one you should worry about. There's no bond like a song.[95]

I can hardly wait to see you. The weather is not better and we probably won't be able to take our walk but I'll find things for you to do. Bring your anagrams. I may be reduced to playing your game since I seem to have none of my own.

What do you think I called you for if not to tell you I loved you? You're supposed to be able to read my mind and that's why I didn't bother to mention it. You're nice, even if you aren't sentimental as I am. I'll have to leave you occasionally after marriage so you can write me you love me – You'll never tell me, I know.

Betty

74. Milwaukee, Monday [April 10, 1933; sent Special Delivery]

Dear Bob –

I was led astray this evening and therefore you may not get a letter until Wednesday. I regret that, but you should be glad to learn that Mr. Jones cooperated by reading to me a chapter on marriage in the book he was currently reading. It turned out to be a light treatment of that subject, but anything I can learn is too little.

In the pleasant haze you create by your presence I forgot to discuss some matters with you. Where am I going to stay this weekend? I wish that I had asked Stewart how he felt about my staying with Nell, but since I haven't I must leave the matter to your good judgment.

I shall be seeing you again on Friday evening shortly before seven. That day should arrive in no time at all – and then three whole days with you.

I think I'm improving in my attitude toward my career. Twice in the past few days I have felt positively kindly toward Mr. Patterson. It must be that love is gradually erasing all the petty meanness from my nature.

This weekend has made me feel so securely happy, instead of frustrated as I sometimes feel after seeing you. I have sometimes thought that you suspect

---

95 Ruth Etting was one of Bob's favorite singers, and he had a large collection of 78 rpm records of early jazz from the 1920s and 1930s. Betty said that one of the ways she impressed Bob initially was knowing all the words to the songs on his records. See "Introduction."

my love if I feel either secure or happy – How can I keep feeling that way after spending a day and a half in that companionable harmony which you inspire. I'm getting into rhetoric in spite of myself. I can't resist trying to describe indescribable feelings. At any rate, I love you and I only feel really complete when you are with me.

Betty

75. Milwaukee, Tuesday [April 11, 1933]

Dear Llewellyn –

I have just spent the evening taking care of a baby with Margaret. Do you consider that a constructive use of time? It seems very simple. I didn't see or hear the baby until its parents came home.

I bought a coat today not to mention a hat. I'm just a touch doubtful about the hat, but I think the coat is a good conservative purchase. I may not be able to wear it if the weather isn't warm, so please don't be disappointed if you see me in the same old clothes. When I buy things nowadays I get panicky for fear you won't like them, even though I know you don't attach undue importance to such things. I really don't care whether I have anything new or not, except that I want to look well for you – That's really true, strange as it may sound –

I certainly do fill up pages with trivial matters. A page and a half on my emotions over buying a coat!

I hope you're busy planning things for me to do during my vacation. I expect to rise at dawn and interview prospective employers until dark. I can't do that without your cooperation. The evenings can well be spent discussing the accomplishments of the day and planning for the next. It is well that I wrote you yesterday of my peace and security. I still have security but you give me no peace. It certainly would be hell to miss you as I do and then be unhappy with you as well. The swell thing about you is that being with you is infinitely more exciting than I ever imagine it will be. How can you be so satisfactory? Show me your worst side – get drunk – I need to be disillusioned. It's not fair to make me love you so much. I can't stand it –

Betty

76. Chicago, [Tuesday] April 11, 1933

Dear Miss Kehler,

Just a line to let you know how much I enjoyed the week-end at your house. Mr. and Mrs. Mills and cousin Doris, (or is she your aunt!), were all very nice to me and I was sorry not to be able to meet the rest of the family.

I enjoyed Counsellor-at-law a great deal and appreciated your taking me to a play which you knew would interest me on account of my profession. The anagrams also were fun and it was awfully good of you to stay home and play them with me instead of gadding about with some of the many beaux whom I know you must be surrounded by, because of your attractive appearance. Not that you have not pronounced intellectual qualities but there are of course only a limited number of us who appreciate a fine mind like yours, especially when it is attached to such a body. I am afraid you may think me overbold when I speak of your body that way but it seems to have aroused my passion.

The truth is, Miss Kehler, that I have been aroused to the point where I should very much like to marry you. I am not well situated at present but a man with my education and experience will prosper eventually and I do not think you would make a mistake in forming a union with me at this time. Although I like Chicago I am willing to come to Milwaukee and seek employment there while we struggle along temporarily on your salary. Let me say in conclusion that I love you and would like permission to call you Elizabeth! Please let me have your decision by return mail as I do not wish to keep in suspense those who are expecting a similar decision from me.

Sincerely yours,

Robert Llewellyn Wright

77. Milwaukee, Wednesday [April 12, 1933]

Dear Llewellyn –

You, too, have a beautiful body, but in spite of that I cannot fully agree to your proposal at this time. Your willingness to live on my salary touches me but I feel that I cannot honorably consent to marriage until I find myself in a position to give you the little comforts of life to which you have been accustomed. I am sure that consideration on your part will find you in the same mind with me.

Though I have no right to ask you to wait for me, and though I want you to consider any other proposals carefully, I do want to caution you against taking such a serious step with someone who perhaps may have more money than I but who will not be able to give you the sincere love and affection of which I feel myself capable. When you have had as much experience as I, you will find that pretty clothes are no solace for a mistaken marriage.

As I say, weigh each prospect carefully. If you find one who, body for body, mind for mind, and income for income compares favorably with me, one who in addition will promise to love, cherish and support you as I shall do when circumstances permit me, I shall be the last to stand in your way. I shall be glad to send you a small gift, even perhaps an occasional necktie at Christmas or for your birthday, though, mind you, I don't promise those.

I wish to ask just one favor of you. Will you postpone your decision until next Friday and let me talk it over with you further at that time? This is too important a decision to be made hastily or alone, and you will still have time for a June wedding and for your shopping and the showers which I know your friends will want to give you.

Your friend and well-wisher,

Elizabeth Bryan Kehler

[written up the side of the page]: P.S. You will forgive me for calling you Llewellyn, I hope. After your letter I am sure that this small intimacy will not be misinterpreted.

78. Chicago, [Thursday] April 13, 1933

Dear Betty,

Why have you shifted to Llewellyn? Not that it isn't my name but the change alarms me because it may have some psychic or numerological significance or something. Do you want me to call you Elizabeth? Don't tell me we have reached the peak of our intimacy and are drifting back to formality.

Seriously, I rather like it, but you should be consistent. On second thought you shouldn't. You should call me by as many names as others do, if not more. After all, I should appreciate being called by my regular names, such as they are, rather than - say - snooky-ookums. Besides, signing different names gives me a feeling of versatility.

I visited Edris today at the hospital and she is returning Saturday with a nurse so you would be a bother there. However, Stewart says that Nell will be glad to have you but I am having him check that tonight with Nell. If worst comes to best you can always sleep with me. Anyway I'll meet you at Grand Ave. at 6:55 P.M. tomorrow for dinner. I probably won't know you in your new clothes so please wear a white orchid. I saw some great pictures of you the other night in your mother's photograph album. The last fifteen or twenty years have done a lot for you. How about appearing in a blue sailor suit with the bowl bob and hair-ribbon so that I can really appreciate you.

If you don't supply me with a picture pretty soon I am going to steal one out of the album. That is unless you can supply me with your presence permanently, in the flesh and when I say in the flesh I mean the flesh – not the spirit. All your spirit does is haunt me when the flesh is not around. And as if that weren't enough to put up with you deliberately unbalance my mind with letters that say you love me. As for my part, I don't intend to tell you I love you until I see you but I can't be unfaithful because if I don't see you I won't live.

Llewellyn

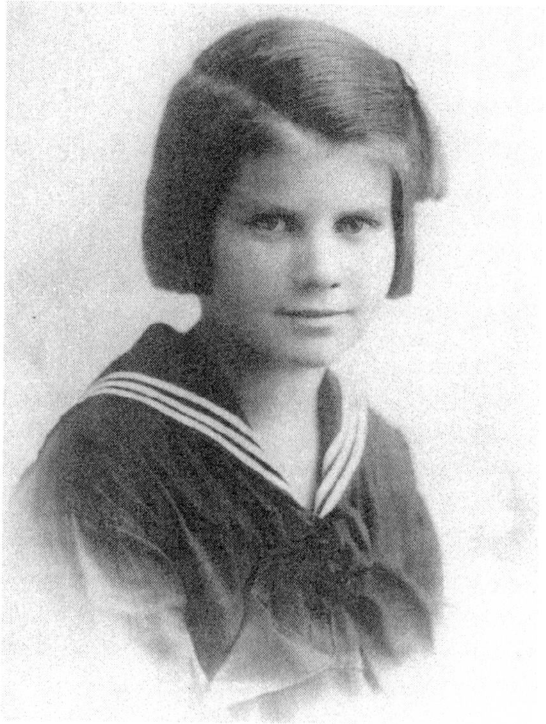

28. Betty in a sailor suit and bob cut (See also Illustration No. 6).

79. Milwaukee, Tuesday [April 18, 1933]

Dear Bob -

I started today an intensive survey of the watch making and repairing trade. It may be fun, who knows? The material is a little scarce but that merely proves the great need for my work.

It was swell being with you for three days, four hours and forty minutes. I wish it could have been forty-nine. Then I might have been satisfied.

Don't forget to give the matter of next weekend your attention.

I can't write you any more now but I'll try to make up for it the rest of the week.

I love you, I love you, I love you -

Betty

80. Chicago, [Wednesday] April 19, 1933

Dear Betty,

Now that you have mastered the watch repairing trade and written a pamphlet about it I am anxiously awaiting news of your conquest of shorthand. I too have been busy, mainly in correcting Miss Johnson's typing mistakes and watching her repeat them with variations. She has now written a bill of complaint five times without failing to omit at least one line in every page each time and I am thinking of killing her. However, I expect to find some time to think up additional tasks for you by the end of the week.

I was offered eight hundred and twenty-five dollars in settlement of a suit yesterday but in order to make my one third pay the cost of marrying you I have fixed the price at three thousand. I turned down the offer with the result that my client may get nothing and I may stay single but you can appreciate the thrill I experience in turning down money these days.

I haven't been able to talk to Stewart yet but will write you about the week-end tomorrow. Maybe I will even confide in you to the extent of telling you I love you. It is possible that I don't because I haven't done anything about the ring yet. We must get someone started on it next week. Don't be so passive. Prod me about it.

Creight Miller is over here and I have just put him to work on the geographical puzzle in an effort to get my money back. He says to give you his best but I won't risk it.

Bob

81. Milwaukee, Wednesday [April 19, 1933]

Dear Bob –

No letter! What does this mean? I would have felt sorry about not writing you earlier this evening were it not for the blank you made in my day. I love you, anyway, damn you –

I had dinner at the Jones' tonight followed by a very interesting conversation with Carol, the communist law student in case you've forgotten, about economies, politics etcetera. I still haven't fathomed the background for her Communistic tendencies but I hope to get to that in the next session.

However, this is all beside the question. Do you still love me and if so why? Tell me about [it] some time. I've heard that you do but I can't seem to make myself believe it.

I gathered all the material I know how to get today – I shall start writing tomorrow. Six thousand seems more than ever like a hell of a lot of words. I checked one of the "My Life Work"[96] series today to see if I were crazy and they seem to be less than two thousand. I think these people are nuts. A shorter pamphlet would cover the ground and be much more suitable for the young and be much more likely to be read. Call Mr. Pugh and tell him what I think, will you, or else tell him to go to hell – I don't care.

Again this is beside the question. May I repeat to you your remark to me as we lay on the bed – what a suggestive phrase – I blush at it – Don't take seriously everything I say, my plaints especially. I'm very glad to try this and I'd be delighted to do something much tougher if it had any possibility of bringing us together sooner. That's the only important thing – and I love you very much. What a cool phrase for my feeling!

Betty

P.S. Write me! I need your letters when I can't love you.

---

[96] R. L. Cooley, the founder and director of the Milwaukee Vocational School, put out a series of vocational pamphlets about different professions under this title.

82. Chicago, [Thursday] April 20, 1933

Dear Betty,

Regardless of the fact that I have received no letter from you today I am going to invite you down for the week-end. Stewart and Nell say it is alright for you to stay with her so I'll meet you at Grand Ave. at 1:53 unless I hear from you to the contrary. I have been trying to write a brief, which has given me writer's cramp, but it seems to make the writing look better. Or can't you read it?

It's a mistake to tell you that I love you before I see you but I'm telling you. You should be made to find it out for yourself each week-end and kept in suspense during the week. This week-end I will prove my love for you by writing your brochure, if I may be permitted to broach it to you. That's what your pronunciation makes me do. I imagine I must keep you in stitches!

Bob

83. Milwaukee, Thursday [April 20, 1933]

Dear Llewellyn –

It's such a beautiful day I should be out playing but instead I'm writing to you. That's what love does for you.

I got weighed today and I have apparently gained three more pounds, making a total of seven. I can't believe it. There is a passage in Sadie Shellow's psychology book which says that love if unmixed with jealousy or fear is the only constructive emotion. She says that one may note the glowing, healthy expressions of a recently married couple. They seem to have gained weight. It is simply the effect of love. My point is that I don't have to get married to have love do me good, and what's more it shows how free my love is from jealousy and the baser emotions. If you marry me I'll be an ox in a year.

Your story about turning down the settlement scares me. I don't know why it scares me, though. I think it's a noble risk to take.

I wish you would think up something for me to do in my spare time. I'm getting tired of idleness and I know I'll have plenty of it if I get married. Incidentally, what are you doing for professional growth?

I love you,

Betty

84. Milwaukee, Monday [April 24, 1933]

Dear Bob -

I was talking to Mary today and she told me she wished that you could be here next Saturday afternoon to play tennis with Porter. She says Porter loves to play and he has a hard time finding someone to play with him. She is also afraid he will brood while she is at the convention. I had thought it would be nice for you to give me a workout on Sunday, so if you do come to Milwaukee you might consider coming in the afternoon so that neither you nor Porter will brood. You may have something better to do to keep from brooding, however.

I meant to ask you what you considered the best procedure for dealing with Mr. Pugh after I finish this pamphlet. I am quite sure that he won't be eager to give me an advance on royalties. I doubt if that is customary in work of this sort. Shall I send it to him, start work on the next one and then attempt to see him the following weekend to make arrangements for some sort of agreement? Give the matter your thought.

It seems absurd that anything should keep us apart in weather like this. I remember feeling exactly the same way in every other kind of weather, especially blizzards. In short, it seems absurd that anything should keep us apart ever. You're such a swell person to have around. I'd like to hire you as a companion with perhaps some of the duties of a personal maid such as undressing me and putting me to bed. I'd be willing to give you board and room and occasional spending money.

I'd love to go to Spring Green[97] as you know, but I'll try to see that you have fun even if you come to Milwaukee. If the weather is nice we can find lots of things to do.

It was an exceptionally nice weekend and I love you.

Betty

85. Milwaukee, Tuesday [April 25, 1933]

Dear Bob -

I am having such a hard time settling down to my professional work that writing a letter seems like relaxation. I should, however, be able to finish up the

---

97 Spring Green, Wisconsin, is the town nearest to Taliesin, Frank Lloyd Wright's residence and school, where Betty and Llewellyn had their first date. See Letters No. 2 and 3, and note 35.

pamphlet tonight and start typing tomorrow. Mr. Merrill is going to let me use his typewriter, so that solves one problem nicely, unless you'd like to type it in your spare time. In my present mood I'll be very happy to get it off my hands, though I have at times enjoyed working on it.

My shorthand books arrived yesterday and I am awaiting the first lesson with almost breathless expectation. I don't believe I've told you before that I decided to take that up, too. I remind myself of Eddie, giving in so meekly to your half-serious advice. I hope you are not similarly disappointed in me for my weakness of character. It is certainly true, though, that the less one undertakes the busier one feels. I haven't felt so ambitious and capable since I was in college. I may turn out to be an efficient instead of a lazy wife if I continue this program.

The time when I will see you next seems very far off, depressingly so. I trust that you haven't given up writing letters. I somehow hope for one on Tuesday though I never get one. That's an unnecessarily plaintive remark. Excuse it, please.

The fact is that I am in a temporary slump and am writing in consequence a dull letter. I'll come out of it by tomorrow and write you a letter radiating cheer and energy, not to mention passion.

In the meantime I love you and I miss you.

Betty

86. Chicago, [Tuesday] April 25, 1933 [Sent Special Delivery April 26]

Dear Betty,

Please note that I always date my letters. The reason for that is that it will enable you to arrange them in chronological order when you publish them. Your letters to me have no dates and will have to be published according to whatever arbitrary arrangement I may decide upon but I don't think it will make much difference. Of course if we published them together yours might be placed in accordance with their relation to mine but this would still leave a considerable number of your letters with no place at all. These might be grouped at the end as an appendix or might be replaced altogether by one composite letter combining the best features of each. Then we could also have tables at the front showing the number of times "I love you" was used by each and supplemental tables showing the frequency of such phrases as "I hate you," "You are a dirty little bum!" etc. The one I am writing will go down in history as the one in which I called you a brazen little hussy, because that is what you are. Why don't you make me a proposition that I can honorably accept?

I can't tell you much about the week-end yet but right now it looks like tennis with Porter. Anyway, have Mrs. Mills get the twin beds ready for us (you and me) as I want to get some rest and we don't seem to be able to sleep on your day-bed.

I will tell you just what to do and say with respect to Mr. Pugh and all your other problems when I see you so please don't keep teasing me to tell you by mail. Remember too that the mere fact that I love you, doesn't give you the right to be so forward and mention things like undressing you. You should be thinking of undressing me.

Bob

87. Milwaukee, Wednesday [April 26, 1933]

Dear Llewellyn –

It almost broke my heart not to find a letter when I got home this afternoon but your Special Delivery arrived shortly after to mend it. It was a kind thought and I appreciate it.

I worked like mad for an hour and three quarters this afternoon and typed some eight pages of manuscript. I hope my speed increases before I finish. I received a pep letter from Mr. Pugh today. He says he will send me a contract soon. I hope it arrives when you're here. I'm not teasing you! I don't want you to write letters like this.

I am longing to know what sort of a proposition you can accept. Can it be that my lack of imagination is restraining you from entering into some particularly happy relationship with me? I hate to think so.

I love you so much that it seems silly to talk about it any more. Why can't I fall back on calling you names, as you do me? Because I'm a much more refined person – that is the answer. Please develop some awful vices, so that I can love you in spite of them. That would be much more fun than this incessant praising your virtues. I'm afraid you'll turn out to be so perfect in our married life that I'll hate you for my own shortcomings.

Anyway, I love you, irreproachable as you are –

Betty

88. Chicago, [Wednesday] April 26, 1933

Dear Betty,

I'm glad to hear that you are finishing that pamphlet in ten days instead of the two weeks you anticipated. Now just think how much less time it will take you when you can write it out in shorthand instead of long-hand.

While you are learning to write more rapidly I am going to teach myself to read faster. The technique I have worked out is to read from the middle of the page to both sides and down rather than from left to right and down. This may result in crossed-eyes but should make me your equal as a reader.

It is really a dangerous thing for you to take up shorthand because if you become proficient I shall be forced to become equally proficient in self-defense. Please don't be good at it.

I just caught myself biting my nails in the throes of composition so perhaps I had better not write you so often. It forces me into bad habits. When I start doing that it is time to stop writing so I'm going to cease just as soon as I have told you again that I love you, that we must be married by May 1 to save my face, that we would be crazy to get married before June 1, that I want to start living with you at once, that I can't live with you until we're married, that I can't live without you, that the fact that I am living without you is inexplicable, that there are no facts other than the one that you love me and that I - how many times must I say it without doing anything about it - love you.

Bob

89. Milwaukee, Thursday [April 27, 1933]

Dear Bob -

I went over to talk to Porter tonight and it seems that Mary's and my tennis idea was a little premature. The public nets are not yet up and when Porter played another person got a net from somewhere and he doesn't know where to get one. They also climbed a fence to get in. Porter says you could climb the fence but he doesn't think you could make a net. He told me to put the facts up to you and let you make your own decision. The park nets may be up by Saturday but in that case you might not be able to get a court.

I am sorry that I led you to believe it was all arranged. Anyway, this sets a new record for me of two letters in one day and enables me to continue telling you how much I love you.[98]

Please don't think from the immediately preceding letter that I don't want to marry you today or tomorrow or any minute you may suggest. I do. No matter what difficulties arise – or delays – there must be no matter of pride involved, that's all. I'll never be disappointed in you no matter what you do. I love you too completely for that. I seem to go over the same ground interminably. I love you, I admire you, I trust you, I want to marry you, I can't live without you. What else is there to say?

I realized with horror today that it will be only ten years until you're forty. We can't waste any more of that than we have to. We won't. I know it. We need each other now and forever.

If there is any logic in the course of this letter I defy you to find it–

Betty

P.S. If you decide not to come earlier, arrive at six at least. I should be here then and I can't wait.

90. Milwaukee, Monday [May 1, 1933]

Dear Bob –

I'm so full of emotion that I can scarcely write you. I want you so much that I feel positive physical pain in being without you. I started the morning, week and month by weeping when I woke and realized you were gone. A rather silly performance but not nearly so silly as our ever having to be apart when we love each other. If this is romance give me anything else, as long as it means being with you constantly, having you completely. The only thing that makes it bearable is knowing that you love me.

It would be better for me probably if you weren't so unfailing in your considerateness and understanding. If you became hurt or cross just once when I deserved it, I might become a better girl. One of the nicest things you ever said to me was the remark about not having to depend upon moods for assurance. It makes me determined to eliminate all but the good moods.

I might as well stop trying to tell you how I feel about you. If I felt less I might come somewhere near expressing it. As it is, I fail miserably.

---

[98] I have not found another letter from Betty for this day in the collection.

I have permission to take next Saturday off. I shall arrive at eight o'clock standard time which I suppose means nine o'clock your time.[99] I don't see any way to make it earlier, but if I can I will. Will you ask Nell if I can stay the extra night with her?

There are two things I'd like to know, but don't strain yourself to find them out. If you should see Marianna Heile,[100] I'd like to know how she got gypped on the writing for royalties that she did. She must have had a similar agreement to the one I am offered. The other is where Peggy Bissell buys shoes.

I love you more than I ever thought I could love anyone.

Betty

91. Chicago, [Monday] May 1, 1933 [Sent Special Delivery May 2, 12:30 AM]

Dear Betty,

So you never get a letter on Tuesday? Let this teach you never to wish for one again. I am going to reprimand you for choosing to have the "curse" instead of a wedding today. Otherwise you might have been able to wake up beside me in bed this morning like the girl in Arno's drawing saying, "Get up, nut! Today is the day we get married."[101]

I feel very much like crying because we aren't married or rather crying because our circumstances haven't improved enough to justify our marrying. This brings up the question of whether they've improved at all. I don't think mine have and the mere fact that the fault is only mine doesn't mean that they

---

[99] At the time of the letters, Chicago went on Daylight Saving Time during the summer months while the state of Wisconsin did not. DST was formally adopted in the United States in March, 1918, when the U.S. was participating in World War I, and observed for seven months in 1918 and 1919. The measure was so unpopular that it was repealed in 1919 and then became a local option. It was continued in a few states and in some cities, Chicago among them. It was re-established nationally during World War II, and then again in 1966, still allowing for local exemptions. <http://www.webexhibits.org/daylightsaving/e.html>, p. 7 "Early Adoption and U.S. Law."

[100] Marianna Heile was the wife of Chick Heile, who gave the party where Bob and Betty first met.

[101] This Peter Arno cartoon is reproduced in *The Complete Cartoons of the New Yorker* (New York: Black Dog & Leventhal, Distributed by Workman Pub., c. 2004). It shows a naked woman in bed next to a snoring man, with the caption "Wake up you mutt! We're getting married today." The editor of the book, Robert Mankoff, says in his Editor's Note that the cartoon "never appeared in the magazine or in any New Yorker cartoon album" although "a lot of people, myself included, are convinced that it's a New Yorker cartoon." He does not say where it did appear.

necessarily will improve. I may go on like this for years. If I don't stop I may go on like this for pages, which would be worse. Anyway I'm going to have you with me again in a few days so it doesn't matter much - except that your leaving me again matters - and there I am back at the starting point - and finish, my love for you.

Bob

92. Milwaukee, Tuesday [May 2, 1933]

Dear Bob -

Your letter pleased, in fact, delighted me. I knew that you would make it if I begged you long enough. I don't understand how you can think the same things I am thinking. Your letter was full of things I wanted to say to you yesterday but hesitated to. It's swell to know we're in accord. Even if we're both sad, I'm glad that we can be sad over the same things.

I have to go to my damn bridge club tonight so I'll also have to stop writing.

If I didn't know that I'll see you Friday I don't think I'd live. I love you.

Betty

93. Milwaukee, Wednesday [May 3, 1933]

Dear Llewellyn -

No letter today. How can I tell whether you still love me when I can't read it at least every night? It's bad enough never to know whether you love me today without wondering about yesterday as well.

Your system is doubtless the best, however. With nothing on my mind and the same old thing on my heart I still continue to write daily letters, the very thing which I swore I would never do - never even want to do - because I'm different. Love has made the same sort of damn fool of me that it makes of every other girl. The only thing that keeps me from talking baby talk and calling you pet names is a very wholesome fear of your disapproval.

I must confess that I have been lazy this week. I have barely started work on the second pamphlet. I hate to waste one bit of effort on something I may decide not to do. I also hate to give up any of the time allotted to thinking about you. That's a full time job in itself and my work at the vocational school has been infringing upon it seriously for some time.

Enough of this foolishness – One more night without you and then I can be foolish with you instead of at you –

Betty

94. Chicago, (No day or date on letter; envelope is postmarked [Thursday] May 4, 1933 and sent Special Delivery)

Dear Betty,

I haven't been able to write you because I ran out of stationery. Rather than stop writing altogether I have decided to use this.[102]

Nell says it will be all right for you to stay with her Friday and Saturday. Jim Cunningham offered the use of his apartment if you aren't afraid to be alone. However, I am afraid that you wouldn't be alone if I would help it.

The weather is not very promising now and what you will bring with you I don't know but please be prepared for some tennis so that we may determine once and for all whether we are going to be able to live happily together.

Bob

95. Milwaukee, Monday [May 8, 1933]

Dear Llewellyn –

I'm a softie! I ache from head to foot. It even hurts me to sit down. It was fun, though, and if you can stand it we'll do it again. I'm talking about tennis, in case you don't understand.

Fate is closing in on us, Bob. Your room has been rented so I'll have to find a new place for you to stay when you come here. If this goes on we'll have to meet in Waukegan and stay at a hotel.

I am enclosing a buck with which I would like you to buy some flowers for Nell and put both our names in. I think you ought to be able to do it for that, though it isn't much.

---

[102] The stationery has his professional letterhead on it (see Illustration No. 25). His letters are usually on personal stationery (see Illustration No. 17a).

At various times I have feared that our love had reached an impasse, that because of the restrictions on our conduct that it must either become static or regress. After this weekend I am convinced that no matter how hampered we are, I for one will continue to love you more each time I'm with you. I wish that I could give you some small idea of what your love and affection mean to me, but I can't. There are no words for what you have done for me or what you are to me.

I don't expect to be unhappy without you this week or any other week if you continue to be as you were this time. If that isn't enough love to last me through five days I'm a spoiled little brat and don't deserve any.

It seems too bad that my parting word to you should have been "nuts", but that's my subtle way of saying "I love you" on L platforms.

Remember that your being out of stationery is no excuse for not writing. Write me on anything, use old wrapping paper, but write!

Betty

96. Milwaukee, Tuesday [May 9, 1933]

Dear Bob -

I'm going to write you just a note because Bobby Jones is sitting here telling me his troubles and I have to listen to them occasionally for old times' sake.

I am full of ambition this week but I don't know when I'm going to get started working for tomorrow night I go to a meeting. However, there are the early morning hours.

Bobby has just told me that I am a lucky devil, meaning, I think, that I have you. He's right and I know it.

I discovered today after writing an apologetic letter to Mother that next Sunday is Mother's Day. I hope you did the same. Where I am going to stay next week puzzles me but you who solve all my problems should certainly be able to solve that.

I love you with all my heart and I can't wait to hear you tell me the same thing, though I know it always.

Betty

97. Chicago, [Tuesday] May 9, 1933 [sent Special Delivery May 10, 1933]

Dear Elizabeth,

Thanks for the dollar. I visited Nell today at the hospital and thought I had the situation well in hand but now you have charmed me into flower buying. Both our names on the card means a two dollar floral display which should fill the room. I'll see that you get credit for the idea as well as the money.

You are going to be a problem this week-end. Nell's mother will be with her but you may be able to sleep on the Carsons' couch. Maybe you had better stay in Milwaukee. Possibly, it would be better for us never to see each other again as I don't see how we can improve on the last week-end - unless we get married. That is the solution. Let's not see each other again until we are married.

There is only one drawback to that plan. We can't get married until you win a set of tennis from me and there doesn't seem to be anyone willing to teach you to do this, but me. I think I had better instruct you by mail.

It looks as though [? illegible] has rented a room for Mrs. Mills. Maybe it will get you paid. I wish they would simply refuse to pay you outright so that I could induce you to leave without assuming any more responsibility than that of trying to feed and house and clothe you. Then if you starved, slept in the street and went ragged you would be comforted by the conviction that you would have done so in Milwaukee, anyway.

What happened to the scheme for getting every Saturday off. Where is your ingenuity? I guess you don't love me.

But I love you regardless. I don't just say I love you; I love you. So, there!

Llewellyn

98. Milwaukee, Wednesday [May 10, 1933?][103]

Dear Bob -

Are you kidding me with this Elizabeth stuff or do you really like to call me that? The reason I address you as Llewellyn at times is because I like it and want to accustom myself to it. I don't want anyone to have a name for you that I haven't, too.

---

103 There is no envelope for this letter.

I am inclined to agree with you that now is the time, if ever, when we ought to give each other up in a supreme romantic renunciation. It's hard to imagine sustaining this peak of emotion for long. I am somewhat sincere in saying this in that for the first time I can see faintly why two people should separate in order not to mar a perfect relationship. However, the more I write the more frightened I become lest you agree with me. All things considered, I'd rather be unhappy with you (ridiculous thought, isn't it?) than romantic without you.

Incidentally, you'll have to think up a better excuse than that tennis idea if you don't want to marry me, and you can't wait until they stop paying me either. I have a pretty good idea when I'm going to get married and I'm not going to tell you until a day or so before. I want it to be a surprise for you.

Don't strain any friendships finding a place for me to stay. If you want to come here I'm sure I can get you a room in the neighborhood. I would prefer to come there but I don't see quite how you're going to manage it.

So I don't love you! That stops me so completely that I can't even tell you I do. Wait 'till I get you near me again.

Betty

P.S. I love you.

99. Chicago, [Thursday] May 11, 1933

Dear Betty,

I call you Elizabeth because I think it is a pretty name and if I thought E. Bryan was I would call you that. Betty, while not a very handsome name, is easy to say and write. So what?

Please don't try to get out of coming down here by mentioning strained friendships. If you don't it will strain ours to the breaking point and it will never blossom into love. In fact I think you should explain to me why you aren't here now. You haven't yet let me know the train to meet but I assume that you will take Friday afternoon and Saturday off.

I am glad to learn that you have a "pretty good idea" when you are going to get married. I wish I could say the same. I hope you will be happy with your husband and that I shall be the first to know. Always remember that I love you.

Bob

100. Milwaukee, Thursday [May 11, 1933; sent Special Delivery the evening of May 12]

Dear Bob—

I was quite despondent today over the thought of our giving each other up after all these months of romance together, so I called Cliff Manor, which is two doors from Mrs. Mills' rooming house, and they will give you a room for a dollar a night. Perhaps I am being forward, but if you do want to see me you may come here. I am expecting to hear from you tomorrow and if you have arranged for me to come to Chicago that's all right.

We will probably be invited to the Cooley's for dinner or something if you do come and if the elusive Joe is about. Margie is planning to have a picnic sometime when you come so that my friends who have been wild for a sight of you for months may meet you. I thought you were my own dark and terrible secret but apparently your name is bandied about by all the girls.

Jean Walker Orr has invited us for supper or tea the evening of May 28th but I'll discuss that some other time. I've used up too much space already on my friends' interest in you.

What can I tell you that I've never told you before? All I can think of are the inane things I don't dare put into writing. I can occasionally slip one in when I'm with you, and then pretend I don't mean it, but I don't want such things in our published correspondence.

I live nowadays almost exclusively in the present and future, but occasionally I become reminiscent. I have such a swell recent past, enough to sustain me if you leave me and I never find anyone else to love me. All the good moments of my life before I met you are scarcely equivalent to one weekend's happiness with you. And this is only the beginning. I love you, Bob. That's not enough. I love you, I love you, I love you.

Betty

[written up side of page] P.S. If I come there I'll arrive at 153 Grand Ave. at 2:53 Daylight Savings. You understand that all things being equal I prefer Chicago, but mainly I want to see you as soon as possible – B.

101. Chicago, [Tuesday] May 16, 1933 [the letter is postmarked (Monday) May 15, 1933 and sent Special Delivery; Bob must have put the wrong date on his letter.]

Dear Betty,

I don't want this to be regarded as a precedent. You won't get a special on Monday simply by being on the verge of tears on Sunday.

But I love you just as much whether you feel like laughing or crying. The really important thing is that I have something to do with the feeling. It is very flattering to have you visibly moved by an emotion that I'm partly responsible for and I feel obligated to arrange an emotional display for you some time. I think tears would be nice but I may put on something even better.

Anyway, we're going to be together again in no time at all and there's only ninety miles between us at any time. In the meantime, please cry your eyes out so that they will be absolutely dry when I see you. Dry and starry. I love you summer, winter, spring and fall but I love you smiling best of all. Poetica erotica!

Bob

102. Milwaukee, Monday [May 15, 1933]

Dear Bob –

Thank you for the letter. I don't feel so badly about my emotional display after reading your poetry.

I didn't intend to write you tonight. I wanted to surprise you, too. You're too quick for me, though. And I can't do it after you exerted yourself for me.

I see no reason why I shouldn't come to see you this weekend if that is your wish. There will probably be nothing special for you to do here.

The next weekend won't be as bad as you expect, as I see it. I talked to Margaret and she is not driving but will go on the train with me. She doesn't want to take the last train back, but will go in the evening sometime and she has no objection to going back alone if I want to stay longer. I don't see why I have to stay with Jean, either, if you don't want me to, by which I mean if you prefer to have me in the neighborhood. Anyway it's only one weekend and while it may have some boring moments for you I think you can take it.

I was just amazed to find a partly finished letter I wrote to you last October in which I thanked you for the pleasant weekend at Taliesin, the first one. I hope I sent one at that time though why I rejected this is beyond me. It sounds very nice.

I still feel very tired and dull but I am truly sorry for my unpleasant performance. If I thought that it would reoccur I should stay here this weekend. If you feel the need of a change in routine which a week's lapse would give you, don't hesitate to tell me. It might do us both good and at the same time be the punishment I deserve.

In the meantime I love you and I wish I had the imagination to think of something especially nice to do for you.

Betty

[written up the side of the page] P.S. I mean what I said about the weekend, but don't jump to the conclusion that I don't want to see you. I do love you, you know. - B.

103. Milwaukee, Tuesday [May 16, 1933]

Dear Bob -

I was just reading a book I like and I had to stop to write you. I love you - really - not in that insistent selfish way that means I want you to pay me a lot of attention. I want you to be happy and I only hope that I'm part of what will make you happy.

You're a strange sort of a guy and I don't understand you. I don't suppose I ever will and I don't want to. I want to spend my life getting alluring glimpses of what you really are, without ever finding out.

Don't let me ever try to change you. I may try to shape you to what I think I want, but if I do you won't be half so wonderful.

This is a letter of inspiration and may be meaningless when it reaches you. Remember, though, that I love you, and you can interpret that to mean anything in the world you wish.

Betty

104. Chicago, [Tuesday] May 16, 1933

Dear Betty,

Your letter shows that we are in perfect accord. I was going to offer to come to Milwaukee this week-end but Jim announced that he was going to Castle Park with Jack Stibbs so what can we do except spend the weekend alone here. Consider your offer to come to Chicago accepted.

I am not willing to let you beg off a week-end now but if, as I fear the fact to be, the late unpleasantness was due to the constant strain you are under in loving and leaving in rapid succession I shall take your application for leave under advisement. When I say unpleasantness I don't mean unpleasantness for me because I was thankful for every minute of you, regardless of how you felt at the moment, but if the reaction at leaving hurts you enough to overbalance the pleasantness of being together, then you shouldn't be subjected to it so often.

It is disheartening and discouraging for me to have you leave me each week-end before we've really had a chance to be together but for my part, I can stand your leaving me for one week better than I can a two week interval. Unless there is an insurmountable obstacle such as sickness I vote no on any two week separation! I shall be glad to dig up the three dollars any time you can't make the financial grade. (Stop making empty gestures Wright! Enclosed find three dollars).

It has just occurred to me that this entire discussion is a little silly. It's quite natural that you should be disturbed at leaving me now and then [several words crossed out, not legible] just as I am at leaving you. We are going to continue to see each other just as often and as much as possible just as long as we continue to love each other. After we're married there may be some occasion for voluntary separations but let's consider the subject closed until then.

Incidentally, when are we going to get married? You have undertaken to fix the date but I don't propose to let you dilly-dally about it.

Anyway, as the songwriters say, if I love because I love you then why do I love you so much?

Bob

105. Milwaukee, Wednesday [May 17, 1933; sent Special Delivery May 18]

Dear Bob -

You're swell! How do you understand me so well? I don't know myself what's wrong with me until you make everything seem right again.

I'm sending the money right back to you because I see no reason why I should take it. I'll wait until I'm broke and then ask you for it, and hope that you aren't broke, too, at that time. I'm tempted to keep it just so you won't do something foolish with it, but I can't.

I knew that Jim was going away and for that reason I rather hoped you'd want me to come. Don't forget this time to have John get dinner for us.

You needn't be afraid to call it the late unpleasantness. It was that. Thank God it's over. I don't need a vacation from you, just a chance to reestablish my self in your and my own esteem.

I plunged into the shorthand last night only to be interrupted by a call saying that seven members of my bridge club were waiting impatiently for me to remember to come. And tonight Danny came over and I haven't seen him for three weeks so we had to talk everything over. Bawl me out, will you?

Anyway - I'm coming to see you this weekend. Please be twenty minutes late so that I can show you how much I really love you. Laugh at me, do everything you can think of, but love me in spite of what I do to you.

Spring is becoming very beautiful in Milwaukee and it gets me. You must come sometime. I want to play in the back yard with you. For the present I'll play in the basement and be very happy doing it.

Have I told you that I love you?

Betty

[written up the side of the page] P.S. I am embarrassed. I forgot this letter this morning. Will you forgive me? Two-fifty-three at Grand Avenue the same as usual. Betty

106. Milwaukee, Monday [May 22, 1933]

Dear Bob –

If you want to make me love you more than ever be somewhat tired and discouraged as you were last night. It makes me determined to devote my life to you.

I wouldn't have gone so deeply into what might be termed the change in pace of our love had I not felt that it was absolutely necessary for me to know what you were thinking and feeling. Your unselfishness makes it a little hard for me sometimes. You have convinced me that you still want to marry me as soon as possible and I'm going to do everything in my power to bring it about. I want it as much as you do, and I think the dangers of waiting are greater than ever.

Don't worry about me or about us. Just remember that I love you and that I'm going to find a way soon to become your wife. After all, if John is spreading stories about our being married it's time to do something.

If you see the Cunninghams this week ask about that job at the University of Chicago.

I hope that your cold is better. Tell me when you're sick so that I can sit home and worry about you instead of going out on blind dates. I want you to need me, even if you have to be sick to do it.

Thank you for my nice yellow dress. I'll have it nicely pressed and perhaps shortened for next weekend.

I've said it before, I know, but please believe that I love you with all my heart. If I could only be with you to tell you that and to take care of you.

Betty

107. Chicago, [Tuesday] May 23, 1933

Dear Betty,

Your letter was a god-send. I lost a motion for a preliminary injunction in the Federal Court yesterday and was a little sick about it because had I been able to put it over it would have forced a settlement of the case, which would have netted me a good sized fee. It was a long shot but was one of the hopes for raising enough money in a lump sum to marry you and I couldn't help counting on it. I am afraid I am a poor loser in these matters because I spent about four hours this evening at the Bar Association library preparing a motion to strike my opponent's answer and a brief in support of the motion, the granting of which will be some slight salve for my feelings but will not dispose of the litigation in my client's favor at this time. This is much too technical for you to pay any attention to but I think you understand that my fee depends on the successful termination of this litigation and that termination has now been postponed for some time.

So what? So it doesn't make the slightest bit of difference to me whether I lose or win a law suit as long as I know you love me. Your letter was encouraging enough to more than balance any temporary set-backs and I feel sure I can pan gold out of some of my pending litigation, given time. The hell of it is I can't make it pay on schedule. I might as well stop kidding myself about starting married life with five or six hundred dollars in the bank.

On the other hand I am not going to run the risk of losing you in the end by literally starving you now in a marriage without money. I love you so much that I can't reasonably see why we're not married already and yet it doesn't seem reasonable for you to even consider the proposition under present conditions. It is a situation where I have everything to gain and nothing to lose and your position is reversed. But I have a feeling deep down that in spite of the fine and lofty sentiments about poverty and marriage I'm going to lure you into the license bureau the first time you weaken in person, as you've already by mail.

Bob

108. Milwaukee, Wednesday [May 24, 1933; sent Special Delivery]

Dear Bob –

You're getting to be more of a problem to me every day. Last night I couldn't sleep for thinking about you.

I've been a good girl this week. I sent in the first shorthand lesson and I've been practising like mad. I hope to get the second one in.

Please don't forget to find a place for me to stay. I will arrive with Margie at two fifty-three at Grand Avenue unless you tell me that some other station is nearer Jean Orr's.

I hope that you won't mind being nice to Margaret for a while and taking her to Jean's. I like to be alone with you, too, but I will appreciate your patience in the matter. She has been entertaining me for some five years and I've done almost nothing for her. Perhaps I shouldn't have mentioned it. You have better manners than I.

I have lots of things I want to talk to you about this weekend. That sounds depressing – like "Elizabeth, I want to talk to you", doesn't it? One of the first things I have in mind is to tell you that I love you. If I attempt to express myself fully on that subject it will take all weekend, because I love you –

Betty

109. Milwaukee, Wednesday [May 24, 1933]

Dear Bob –

I'm glad my letter helped. If I can't keep you from discouragement I don't know what I'm good for. I'm afraid my last letter was rather matter of fact but it was only so because I want to tell you in person what I'm thinking. I can assure you that as usual we are in perfect accord.

I obtained the name of a place where we may possibly have a ring made and I'm going to investigate it tomorrow if I can possibly do so. This may strike you as rather ironical at a time when you perhaps have no money to buy one but I think it's a step in the right direction.

I am going to say something which I have said so often that it may have lost emphasis, but you must believe me. I love you more than I ever have before, and I'm determined to translate that love into action in the near future.

Please don't be discouraged. The breaks can't be against us indefinitely, and even if they are we aren't going [to] let them stop us. Don't talk about losing me through any circumstance. You can't. I love you too much.

Betty

110. Milwaukee, (no date or day on letter; the envelope is postmarked [Thursday] May 25, 1933, and sent Special Delivery)

Dear Bob –

I got a special from Jean Orr this morning suggesting that we all go to the Fair. She also says she has been unable to find a man for Margaret and wants to know if your roommate would be interested.

I'm just sick about it because I know you don't want to go and I certainly don't enjoy going places when you don't want to. But apparently if we don't go and get some one else to go with us, we spoil the whole idea.

She wants me to let her know so I am writing that I have put the idea up to you. I don't see what else I can tell her.

Love, Betty

[written up the side of the page]: P.S. Don't get the idea that I'm interested in going. I want to be with you and besides I've got a cold. However, I want you to make the decision. It's all right either way.

Part Four: Taking The Plunge Despite All Odds

Letters 111–144, May 29–July 12, 1933

111. Milwaukee, Monday [May 29, 1933, sent Special Delivery]

Dear Bob -

I feel practically well today. I went to work, of course, but I'm going to be very careful of my health tomorrow. I feel too darn well as a matter of fact. I miss you too much. I may have to get sick in self defense or I'll come running down to Chicago.

I couldn't see Mr. Cooley today which was a great disappointment. I can't wait to burn my bridges (please note spelling).

I shudder to think of what I'm about to do to you, killing you with a kiss is what it amounts to, but I shudder still more at the thought of living without you much longer.

This is the last time I'm going to express any compunction. It's your fault anyway. You can't love me as you do on the weekends and expect me to remain sane. I hereby place all responsibility on you.

You can make me leave the house two or three evenings a week because you're bored with me and I'll still love you. Even the picture of you sitting in stony silence for meal after meal while the tears drop upon my unbuttered bread fails to shake my resolution. Just give me poverty and abuse - that's all I ask.

Porter says he'll play tennis with you Sunday if you like. He thinks he's pretty good now. You have to get up at eight, though, if you don't want to wait, and you can play for only half an hour if anyone is waiting. I'd like to play, too, but I probably won't be in condition.

I'm going to spend tomorrow on shorthand, jewelry pamphlet, sewing and so forth in an attempt to sublimate my overwhelming emotion. By the way, I got the first lesson back with many errors but she marked it excellent and said I showed a fine grasp of the theory. Perhaps that's the routine preliminary encouragement. I love you more and more and more.

Betty

112. Milwaukee, Tuesday [May 30, 1933]

Dear Bob –

I've actually worked all day long, starting out by reviewing a large volume entitled "Statistical Procedures in Public Employment Offices", and spending the rest of the day on shorthand and sewing. I've expended a prodigious amount of labor on my old white coat with the net result that it looks just the same but is neater inside where no one will see it. And now I'm lonesome for you.

I just went out in the back yard and noted that the tennis courts are empty, though it is still light. Perhaps they're closed.

I wish I had seventeen more days like this and I might get something done. On the other hand I probably wouldn't. I'd be mooning over you.

I could hardly believe that we wouldn't see each other today but I'm glad we didn't. Perhaps we're getting somewhat practical as we'll certainly have to.

I have more respect for Jim Cunningham than ever if he picked up shorthand in a few days. It's just like learning to write all over again. My hands just don't make the things I want them to.

I forgot to tell you how nice it was of you to invite Margaret for dinner. I appreciated it very much. You always do just what I want you to without my having to ask for it.

Tell Jim that the price of the cottage is twenty bucks a week. My family finally got around to telling me.

If my letter sounds trivial and matter of fact it's because I want you so much that I'm afraid to let myself go. If I didn't know you love me I'd die. I love you.

Betty

113. Chicago, [Tuesday] May 30, 1933 [sent Special Delivery May 31]

Dear Betty,

Your special[104] makes me feel very guilty. While you were working I played tennis and drank beer, if you weren't kidding me.

There was no dollar excursion, as you doubtless know, and I have got to begin saving some money so I stayed here, as you also doubtless know. However, I am going to see you Saturday. If you still have a cold I may be forced to severe measures.

It was really a great relief to have you commit yourself so definitely to marrying me but on the other hand I can't help feeling just a bit frightened by my responsibility in the matter. But love conquers all, even fear, and I love you and fear nothing – as long as you love me.

Bob

114. Milwaukee, Wednesday [May 31, 1933]

Dear Bob –

I have just read your letter which rather worries me. Sometimes I think I'm a fool for imagining that you hold things back from me for fear of hurting or discouraging me, and sometimes I'm sure it's true. I don't like to keep howling at you to discuss things with me, but I do feel it necessary to know what you think. If you are afraid and don't see how we can accomplish marriage at this time you should have told me so last week, but of course it is not too late now. You know, if you have any faith in me at all, that I will wait for you forever. My decision was based on the fact that you apparently were eager to marry me immediately but were afraid for my sake and that I was eager to marry you but was afraid for your sake. That being the situation it seemed to me that we ought to stop being over ambitious for each other's financial security and be happy though poor together. You are much more familiar than I with your financial situation and the expenses we will have

---

[104] See the last paragraph of Letter No. 111, sent Special Delivery on Monday May 29, where Betty says "I'm going to spend tomorrow on shorthand, jewelry pamphlet, sewing and so forth...." Memorial Day was celebrated on May 30 until the National Holiday Act of 1971, calling for it to be celebrated on the last Monday in May, to ensure a three-day weekend for Federal holidays.

and it's absolutely up to you to make the decision. I have no guarantee that I won't be a serious and permanent liability to you, though of course I hope to contribute my share. I can't urge you too strongly to tell me if you think we ought to wait. You can't possibly lose me that way or any other way unless you yourself want to.

I talked to Mr. Cooley today and also to Mr. Patterson because he asked me to, but there is nothing irrevocable about that. You were right in that both of them are willing for me to get married during my vacation and work until the first of September. I would then be entitled to vacation pay, but not if I left before the year is up. I told both of them that I could not definitely decide about it until I found out what the pay situation was. They will mention it to no one and when I decide on the date I will sign a resignation for September first. That is all there is to that.

2. [page 2 of the letter]

We had a meeting tonight to discuss the "baby bond" situation which will mean a lot to you and me in one way or another. Bonds secured by tax warrants go on sale tomorrow. If the sale is successful, which should be apparent in a few weeks, we will probably be paid cash in full for the three months. If it is not successful, we will receive baby bonds which of course will not be as useful, but I may be able to borrow on them. If I do receive cash we will be in a pretty good situation I think, but that's just a matter of speculation now.[105]

There may be hell ahead of us, darling, and if you see it and I don't tell me. I'd much rather have you do that now than to live with you and see the results of my romanticism wearing you down.

If I haven't gotten my ideas across in all this writing I never will, so I'll shut up. I'll see you Saturday anyway and I love you no matter what you decide to do about me. Whether you like it or not we'll have to talk about such things still more, and you can brace yourself for it in the meantime.

It would be nice if you would tell me when you are coming so that I can be sure to see you promptly.

---

[105] See n. 112 and n. 120. "Baby bonds" were created during the Hoover administration to reduce hoarding and expand credit. At that time, they were $100 bonds at 2 % for one year, with the right to redeem them on sixty-days notice (*The Crash and Its Aftermath: A History of Securities Markets in the United States, 1932–33* by Barrie A. Wigmore [Westport, CT: Greenwood Publishing Group, 1985], p. 313).

I did work yesterday but I don't care whether you did or not. It wasn't from choice but from lack of opportunity to do anything else. What happened to the work you had to do?

I have a swell idea for the niche but you'll have to wait two weeks to find it out.

I'm going to try to get two Saturdays off in June.

I won't promise not to have a cough next Saturday but I won't be browbeaten by you if I do, do you understand?

[a series of shorthand symbols] That means "I can go in an hour" which is still my favorite sentence though I know lots more.

I love you –

Betty

115. Chicago, [Thursday] June 1, 1933 [sent Special Delivery June 2, 1933,12:30 AM]

Dear Betty,

There you go! Just as I am nicely settled about our marriage you reopen the question. Once and for all time let me say that we are going to get married in July, even if I've only got the two dollars necessary for a license. Whether you work until September 1 in Milwaukee will depend upon how much of a sacrifice will be involved for you in coming down here before that time. I am glad you talked to Messrs. Patterson and Cooley and my understanding is that we are not only going to be married but living together here not later than September 1. If I can possibly arrange it you will be thumbing your nose at Mr. Patterson before that time.

Eleanor Samuels, the girl who does statistical work at the University of Chicago and draws a hundred and fifty a month for it is leaving there July 1 to get married. They are going to replace her but two of the local girls are being pushed for the vacancy by their respective professional sponsors. Edris has taken the matter up with Prof. Linn on your behalf and you may have a chance to talk to someone about the job next week. The hirer is Mr. Donald Schlesinger. If you know anyone who can put pressure on him go to work on them. This is a very long shot but worth a lot of effort.

I forgot to tell you when I boasted about loafing on Tuesday that I worked until nine thirty Monday night. So there! But I still feel guilty about your slaving for me on a holiday. I would much rather have you cure your cough.

I saw a rather attractive gold wedding ring at Peacock's today for $8.50 but I am still going to try and get one made. I'll try and have something for you to look at next week. It seems to me that a long time has elapsed since I've done anything concrete to demonstrate my love for you but you don't really seem to care. I think you should ride me about my neglect. Anyway, I'm going to take your train-ride for you Saturday. I can't tell you now when I'll reach Milwaukee except that it will be as soon as possible.

Bob

116. Milwaukee, Monday [June 5, 1933?]

Dear Ll-

I found it a very satisfactory and inspiring weekend. I am more than ever convinced that my happiness lies in living with you, and more than ever determined not to let circumstances beat us. Not only in character but in temperament you are the perfect man for me. I'm not going to let circumstances crowd me, but I am going to create some favorable ones for us. As long as we are in such harmony of mind, we'll find a way to get married soon, I know.

Mary told Pat today that she was going to leave and he thought she was going to have a baby. He doesn't now, though. I guess she'll leave in two weeks, which was quite a blow to him. He's going to try to get someone with a master's degree to do my filing and someone with executive ability equal to his to take Mary's place. I guess I'm a cat.[106]

Mr. Winkel wants the vacation schedule made up this week so I'll ask for the last three weeks in August. There's really nothing they can do about it even if it isn't convenient since I will be leaving permanently then. If we find that we can get married sooner I think the thing to do would be to take a long weekend and subtract that from my vacation. My only hope is that the last of August won't crowd you too much, but that's something we can only speculate about. If things don't break for us I can always go home for a while, so don't worry about it.

---

[106] Betty seems to mean she is being "catty," by being sarcastic about the extraordinary qualifications her employer will look for in people to replace her and her co-worker Mary.

I hope that we can get some information about Miss Samuel's prospect so that this Saturday won't be wasted as far as job hunting is concerned. I'm putting in my extra time, though I haven't mentioned the Saturday idea to Mr. Patterson.

I always think of so many things to talk to you about when I'm away, but talking seems superfluous when we're together.

I'm going to work hard on my shorthand and I love you.

Don't go to the Fair without me just because it's nice weather.

Your true love, E.

117. Milwaukee, [Tuesday] June 6, 1933 [sent Special Delivery]

Dear Llewellyn -

I spent half of yesterday looking through a University of Chicago bulletin trying to find Donald Schlesinger for Mr. Rasche. The nearest was Donald Slesinger, Professor of Law. Is this the guy? I'm disappointed in you for giving such inadequate information. It seems more like me. Mr. Rasche, however, promised to write.

Mr. Patterson has given me next Saturday off and says he will see about the other one. He doesn't like the idea of two much but I think he'll come around.

I hear that the vacation schedule is usually planned the last week of school which is next week. We'll have to decide this week, therefore. It looks as though there may be more argument over my taking it in August than in July. Everyone wants it in August.

As you can see I haven't anything very significant to tell you. I feel inhibited in an office, even when I'm all alone. But I do love you a great deal. You were just a little more perfect than usual this weekend. See that you're always more perfect than usual.

I'll see you Friday night and I love you.

Betty

118. Milwaukee, [Tuesday] June 6, 1933

Dear Robert -

I hope you got a letter today. I meant you to, though I was invited out for dinner and didn't get it written last night.

I'm busy as a little beaver or bee, just as you wish, getting my old clothes together to be given away – those I can't make over on the long winter evenings. If I thought you wouldn't be shocked I might come down this weekend with a load of my belongings. A few books won't shock you, will they? Perhaps that's safest.

I still have the feeling occasionally that I'm cutting your throat, but I have to do it.

I haven't a great deal to report. The pay situation looks bad though I still believe I'll get a check on July 1st.

I love you,

Betty

119. Chicago, [Tuesday] June 6, 1933 [sent Special Delivery]

Dear Betty,

I hope you didn't have Mr. Rasche write to Professor Slesinger. The name Schlesinger was very carefully spelled out for me. I'm afraid you're losing faith in me.

I haven't much to report but am enclosing a dollar for the room rent. I remembered forgetting to pay you as soon as I left the house and could hear you saying "well, I guess he is preparing me for my job of supporting him" or did you forget to pay Mrs. Mills?

Please let me know whether you're coming for dinner Friday. You can't come too soon and you may come too late. Not that I'm planning anything dangerous but to be apart from you and separate often seems to make me desperate. What single letter takes desperate. See solution on other side.

Love, Llewellyn

(on other side): s makes datepress, of course, stupid!

120. Milwaukee, Wednesday [June 7, 1933; sent Special Delivery]

Dear Llewellyn –

I had hoped that you would ascertain the exact name, title and address of this guy and let me know, but I realize you have other things to do, and I have now found out, first, in the Chicago bulletin, second from a letter I got this afternoon. He is Dean Donald Slesinger, an associate dean of the social science division. Please note spelling.

The letter I got is as follows: "Dean Slesinger will not be in Chicago on Saturday, July 10 [she must mean June 10]. He suggests that you leave your name and Chicago address with me if you care to call at the office during his absence." Signed Jean Schneider, office manager. I can't see what I gain by leaving the aforementioned things, but I suppose I had better do it. Since I am not sure that I can get both Saturdays off, do you think I had better waive this one, and try to see him the next week? Please advise immediately.

I might try to get Friday afternoon off, if you found out that I could see him then, but this is junior transfer week and I imagine I would encounter some opposition.

If I come as I have planned, I shall arrive at Grand Avenue shortly before seven your time,[107] and since I leave Milwaukee at four, I'm afraid you'll have to give me dinner. If I come Saturday I shall arrive at the usual time, 2:53.

I think it might be a good idea to find out, if you can without too much difficulty, whether I could see him Friday & if so what is the latest time I could do so, and write or wire me what time I would have to leave here to make it, where I should get off, etc. I can then try to accomplish it.

This sounds like a formal and even forbidding letter, but it's the effect of hot weather and my anxiety over Dean Slesinger. You're still the only love of my life and I want to see you as soon as possible, but we mustn't turn down any good opportunities.

What about simply telling me you love me, instead of threatening to enclose dollars?

Betty

---

[107] Chicago was on Daylight Saving Time, but not Milwaukee. See n. 99

121. Chicago, [Tuesday] June 13, 1933 [sent Special Delivery June 14,1:00 AM]

Dear Betty,

I refrained from taking in the Fair on a pass tonight as a result of your warning although I haven't yet received my tickets. If I never get them you will have to supply passes.

If you are really in earnest about job interviewing for Saturday I'll have mother try and make an appointment with Mrs. Lurie for you. I haven't heard anything more about the calculating machine job but there are plenty of places to go if you want to spend your time that way.

Don't you think it's a little bit early to start talking about going home to your mother. That will doubtless be your threat after the first few weeks of marriage and we are going to get married, make no mistake about that, in spite of your vague talk.

The enclosed folder shows that I have been giving serious consideration to our honeymoon. I was all set to take you on the three day "cruisette" but the Geo. M. Cox sank about a week ago. However we can ride out into the lake and back on the Isle Royal for a dollar.[108]

Don't give me any talk about not getting Saturday off. My understanding is that Mr. Patterson is now definitely under your thumb. Anyway, I'll meet you at seven o'clock Friday night if you still love me as I love you –

Bob

122. Milwaukee, Tuesday [June 13, 1933]

Dear Bob –

---

[108] Enclosed in the letter is a two-sided travel brochure stamped by "Arthur W. Wolfe, "Wolfe Way" Tours, 110 S. Dearborn St, Chicago," the same office building where Bob worked. The brochure advertises the "Wonder Cruises" of the Isle Royale Line in Chicago, including a three-day weekend "cruisette" for $18.50 between Chicago and Mackinac Island, aboard the S.S. *Geo M. Cox*. The *Chicago Daily Tribune* for Friday June 2, 1933, has a photo, taken from a passing ship, of the *Geo. M. Cox* sinking, with the caption: "Chicago Steamer Sinking After Running on Reef; 124 Rescued." It goes on to say that the ship went aground "last Saturday" (which would have been May 27,1933) "on Rock of Ages near Isle Royale in Lake Superior" and that "[f]our persons were injured in the wreck."

I have just had a pleasant evening but haven't gotten any work done nor my letter to you written. Mrs. Lindsay invited me to dinner and took Mary and myself to the Cudahy which is a place you and I should have found in our reckless days. Mary will be gone the weekend after next and I imagine I shall miss her quite a bit.

I have been working very hard at the office and have had to stay overtime whether I wanted to or not, but I don't think I shall press the Saturday off unless there is a definite reason for it. I shall ask, however.

My mind is going round and round to no great purpose. I think about you and myself and money and giving you a honeymoon and there's no point to it. All we can do is wait. It has occurred to me that if the new cottage at Lake Ripley isn't rented we could spend a week there. The trouble is that we couldn't count on it because under the circumstance I wouldn't want to ask my family to give up any chance of renting it. Would you consider going there? I know they'd love to let us have it, because it's the only thing they could do for us. We'd be alone and the beds are swell. I didn't mean that the way it sounds but it doesn't matter.

I'm nuts tonight and I can't write you a good letter, but I love you so much I need your sane and calming influence. You're calming to me mentally at least. When I'm with you I know everything will be all right even when I'm having my worst mental spasms.

I meant to ask you more about Martha Botsford and what I might have become without you. Remember to tell me.

I hope that I get a nice soothing letter from you tomorrow. I love you immeasurably and I wish I were with you.

Betty

123. Chicago, [Wednesday] June 14, 1933

Dear Betty,

I am enclosing a clipping designed to keep you from becoming conceited. You are apparently quite conventional but with this difference.

While Miss Blake's girls apparently just talk and write about it you are actually going to do it.[109]

How come no letter? Are you disciplining me for something? If so please do it by writing me a letter and bawling me out instead of ignoring me.

I haven't anything to report except that I love you more than I ever did before and saw Stewart on the street today. He says Nell is getting a divorce this week and they may get married next month too. I told him I wanted to see her make an honest man of him.

See that you do the same for me.

Bob

With (as Marian Harris used to sing) Love, Lahauhve

124. Milwaukee, Wednesday [June 14, 1933]

Dear Bob –

Your letter saved me from complete despair. All I need is to have you put down in writing or say out loud that we are going to get married. Don't forget to do it or I'll go crazy because I don't dare mention it after my deserved reproof last week, and I know that I shouldn't anyway.

I've been in an absurd panic all day. Two people have told me they didn't think we'd get paid the first and if we do I'm afraid I won't have a cent by the time of my vacation – You can see how ridiculous my thinking is. Mr. Patterson has spread the word that I am leaving and is making plans to fill my job and that also puts me in a panic, because it leaves me completely at your mercy. At the same time I want so much to leave, even regardless of you – that's wrong. I can't imagine any situation without you. You're the whole reason for everything – for my very existence. You will probably be

---

[109] The original enclosure is found in the letter. Doris Blake's advice columns on marriage appeared frequently in the *Chicago Daily Tribune* during the period of these courtship letters. The article is entitled "Girl Greater Altar Gambler than Most Men," and the author reports receiving daily letters from women who want to go ahead and get married despite their future mate's not having a steady income, while the men in question want to postpone marriage until their financial situation is more stable. Doris Blake advises that these women "gamblers" are making a mistake they will regret, and believes that the man will not respect himself nor will the woman respect him if she continues to have to support him.

able to detect from this how selfish my thoughts are, and that's what makes me so ashamed. I've cut myself loose from the little security I had, and it makes me frantically and selfishly eager to have you marry me, so that I may regain some confidence in my future. The only proper retort for you is to tell me now that marriage is a compromise and that you refuse to jeopardize our love that way. I recommend that to you as a solution.

In spite of the fact that your letter made me very happy, it also unsettles my mind. I have so much work to do that I have decided not to ask for this Saturday, but a later one, unless you write me that I have an important appointment. I really am snowed under, so don't make an issue of it, but write me tomorrow whether you think it's necessary. Mr. P. is not under my thumb and I don't think he'd give it to me anyway. I refused to do something for him on the grounds that I was too busy and that's something his mind can't comprehend.

I love you - perhaps not as much as you do me because I keep burdening you with my fears, but in my inadequate way I love you almost more than I can stand.

Betty

125. Milwaukee, Thursday [June 15, 1933]

Dear Bob -

I'm going to call you tonight but I've decided to write you anyway because you're such a nice boy and I love you so much.

Of course I wasn't disciplining you. I must have mailed it at the wrong time but I never play games with you that way. The only reason, or the main reason, I write every day is because I can't bear to think of you sticking your hand into that noisy mailbox and being disappointed.

I'm so sorry I made that foolish remark about the Fair. I wish you had gone. It's getting hot again and I may not even want to go if you have the tickets. Why do you pay so much attention to the silly things I say?

Now that the time is getting near I can hardly wait to see you though you may not think so after I call you. I love you.

Why did you say Stewart may get married next month, too? I thought we were getting married in August.

The folder you sent me was very intriguing. It's too bad the ship sank. Did it sink with people? I'm getting like Mary. I don't think I want you to get off land because something might happen to you. The part I liked, though, was the repetition throughout of six meals a day. What could be nicer for me?

I cashed your dollar last night feeling like a criminal, but I had to do it or go without my dinner. I wish that I could know what will happen to it. Why didn't you put your full name and address on it? Are you ashamed of our love?

I refuse to comment on the clipping. To hell with Doris Blake! Everybody around here is doing it with much less security than we have. You'll have lots of company if you want to regret it. And furthermore, I refuse to comment on it.

Don't worry, darling, and reduce life to simplicities as you used to. Now that I'm converted I don't want to see you slip. I love you.

Betty

126. Milwaukee, Monday [June 19, 1933]

Dear Bob –

Leaving you last night in that state was almost more than I could bear, when I wanted so much to take care of you and found myself only an additional burden to you. I wasn't as kind to you as I wanted to be, but it's so hard for me when there are people around to show you how much I do love you. I hope that you are feeling better now. You must feel well whether you want to or not, or I shall die of sympathetic agony.

Pat stayed away from me nicely today and if he continues my work will be in good shape by the time he leaves Friday. I'll try to get Saturday after next off and accomplish big things.

I got a nice note from Mr. Jerome today saying he was out of town when my letter arrived but that his assistant wrote to Mr. Schlesinger and that he had written since. I bet that guy's sorry he didn't hire me now that he knows what a great girl I am.

I'll write my letter to the Bell Telephone Company this week, and possibly to McGraw Hill. If you can think of any other good prospects please write me of them, because I'm very serious about this matter now, even though I was a little slow at getting to it.

Rags and Rea will probably be here before you are next weekend. They are to drive us out to Waubeka. There's no hurry about getting out, however, so come when you can and if you know beforehand let me know the train you are coming on. I might even meet you.

The only other thing I have to say is that I love you more than myself, which is quite a lot, and no matter how I act you must know that that's all I'm thinking. And what's more I'm going to see to it that you're never sorry you married me. I'll be so nice and so helpful and so productive of income that you won't believe I'm the same problem child you used to know. I love you and I want to be with you every minute of my life.

Betty

127. Chicago, [Tuesday] June 20, 1933

Dear Betty,

It seems that the new beer is intoxicating in fact, at least when combined with the hot sun and Marianna's alcohol. I am very much ashamed of myself for giving you such a bad evening. This next week-end you can protect yourself by instructing Margaret not to serve me with anything to drink.[110]

Rumor has it that Stewart and Nell are going to be married at the end of this week. Have you been advised? It looks as though he may be the proprietor of a Lake Forest harem. However, I'm still planning on visiting you in Milwaukee as I haven't been invited to the wedding. We had better combine on a present as it looks as though they're going to be in a position to combine on us.

---

[110] 3.2 % alcoholic beer was approved for public consumption by federal legislators in March 1933, and it was launched officially on April 7 of the same year. There are many articles about it in the *Chicago Daily Tribune* in March and April of 1933, including, on April 4, 1933, an amusing column by Westbrook Pegler, one of Bob's favorite columnists (See n. 50). Another interesting article on the subject appeared on p. 1 of the April 12, 1933 *Tribune* titled, "Is 3.2 Beer Intoxicating? Magistrate Decides It Is," recounting a fine for intoxication imposed on a driver involved in an accident who "testified he had drunk the new beer exclusively."

Last week-end I loved you for your endurance and forbearance. This week-end I want to love you for your discipline.

Bob

128. Milwaukee, Wednesday [June 21, 1933]

Dear Bob -

Margaret took me out to Waubeka yesterday to swim and I thus did not write a letter to you. Do you blame me? That reminds me to tell you to bring your suit with you next weekend.

If there is anything to forgive you are forgiven and I have no intention of disciplining you this weekend. My only feeling was anguish over my inability to make you feel better and your apparent inability to explain what your trouble was.

I am excited over Stewart's approaching marriage. I hope that he does do it as soon as possible, but don't forget you're coming here no matter what my brother does. Your idea about the wedding present is excellent, but what will we use for money?

There was a very cheerful article in the paper this morning to the effect that the city expected to pay all its back salaries in July, and hoped to pay one before the fourth. I don't think it means much but I have recovered from my worrying spell and feel very cheerful about it myself.

I have just written to the Bell Telephone Company and to the McGraw-Hill Company. If you don't have some more ideas I'll be out of employment.

I got a letter today from the Federal Reserve Bank stating that they could give me no encouragement but if I wished I could call for an interview any morning except Saturday between eight and eight-thirty. There you have it. I'd like to do it, but how can I? I also got a letter from Mr. Pugh who wants to know what the hell I am doing by return mail. I have not answered it yet but I shall.

Please think hard about people - companies - for me to write. Time is precious. I can't let you marry me until I have sent out at least a thousand letters and I'd like to marry you. Why? Because I love you, that's why.

This is your name in shorthand. [two shorthand symbols] Bob Wright. I also can write many other important things.

Betty

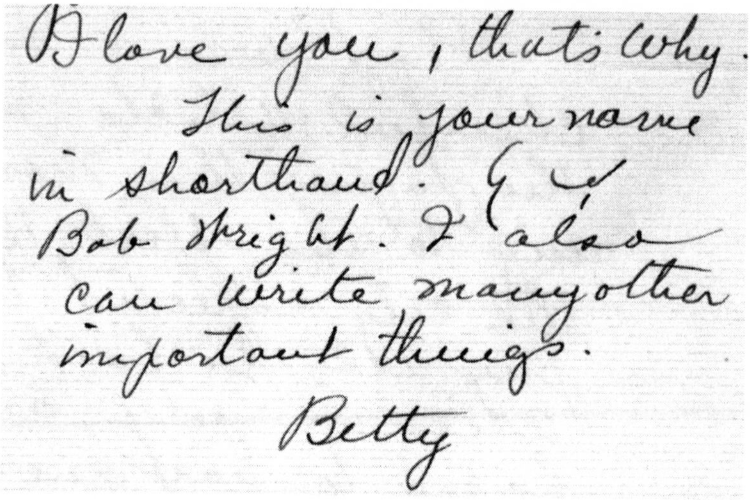
I love you, that's why.
This is your name
in shorthand.
Bob Wright. I also
can write many other
important things.
Betty

29. Letter No. 128, last paragraph, where Betty writes Bob's name in shorthand symbols

129. Chicago, [Wednesday] June 21, 1933

Dear Betty,

I finally got my book of world's fair tickets but promptly turned them over to mother so I wouldn't be tempted to use them before you get here. She is going to use seven over the week-end which I sold her and the proceeds of the sale have helped to buy you a birthday present which I shall bring with me this week-end as it would be silly to wait till July 21 to start using it. Don't get excited because it's not a ring and I'm not at all sure you'll like it but if you don't, then you have plenty of time to make me buy something else.

Mother tells me that Dave is planning on going to Arizona permanently around the first of September and will sell or store his Gary furniture so it looks as though we might be able to do some of the storing. Mother offered to let us have her grand piano but I think that is an item we won't have room or use for. She has written John about the beds but it may be a struggle to get them. Maybe we will have to learn to sleep in the same bed.

I am having my pants cleaned for the week-end but there is no way of keeping them in press so I shall probably appear wrinkled but sanitary on Sunday. I don't know yet what time I can arrive but will wire you. I wouldn't want you to make the trip to the station to meet me unless I get in early enough so that you can go direct from work or luncheon between the school and station.

Your last letter excited me very much and if you persist I don't know whether I can restrain myself, even in the presence of your friends, from exchanging loving for love.

Bob

130. Milwaukee, Thursday [June 22, 1933]

Dear Bob –

Sometime I am going to cast off all inhibitions and address you not as "dear Bob" but as darling or sweetheart or perhaps even "you – " like the man in the New Yorker article which you sent me in the old sane days when I thought, too, that sentimentality was a horrid thing. For after all you are my darling and also my sweetheart, two facts which no preliminary formality can disguise. You can see what a somewhat inhibited weekend has done for my letters. I shudder to think of what I may do to you on July 1st if this weekend is also inhibited, or I am, as I fear I may be.

The truth of the matter is that I love you in no delicate way but with a robust passion, and I don't see how I am going to control it until Saturday morning. If I see you in clean pants I know I can't bear it. I'll bite large holes in them in my excitement.

I'm somewhat appalled at your buying a birthday present for me. I meant to tell you that in spite of my foolishness I wanted nothing but a wedding ring or the prospect of one. I hate to think that my mother's bad planning of my birth date will set my marriage back by so much as a day. I am, however, counting on you to produce something which cannot be returned, and which I will therefore have to gracefully accept. I love you for wanting to give me something almost as much as I'd love you if you weren't able to.

I plan to stay downtown to meet you if you come at one or before, and if you come later I think I can drive down with someone to meet you, so you really don't need to let me know, unless you come later than two, which I am assuming you won't.

I have made the great experiment and I am sitting waiting for my hair to dry and hoping that I may get some food before morning. If I have a large cold you'll know it's because I'm trying to be beautiful cheaply.

I love you, I love you, I love you, and you may take me to the World's Fair.

Betty

131. Milwaukee, Monday [June 26, 1933?]

Dear Bob –

Milwaukee is all agog over your being such a handsome brute and also over your being a full-sized man. I'm so proud of you. I feel justified for having injudiciously remarked to Margaret once that I thought you were beautiful.

I am very stiff from baseball, I think, perhaps from croquet.

I read a book today on how to get a job during the depression. It says letters are of little or no avail. Out of five hundred letters one young man sent out he received thirty-five replies, all stating that there was no work. Nevertheless I shall keep on.

I want to save my Saturday morning for a time when I will job hunt enthusiastically. Right now I feel like necking and nothing else, even in this hot weather. And also I have a small desire to come on my birthday, even though I have my nice birthday present, because I don't like to eat dinner alone on that sacred day.

Thank you again for my present. I shall try to justify it by my performance on the tennis court next week.

I love you so much. Set aside this weekend entirely for me and don't let anyone inveigle us into a mob unless you're sure it's worthwhile.

I'm so tired I can't spell but I do love you.[111]

---

[111] In writing "worthwhile" at the end of the preceding paragraph, Betty left out the "th" and had to insert it above the line.

Betty

132. Chicago, [Tuesday] June 27, 1933

Dear Betty,

The week-end didn't tire me as much as it did you. I feel much healthier for it and enjoyed the exercise as well as meeting your pals. It must have been the strain of having me around other people. If you will supply me with Mrs. Cooley's initials and address I should like to write her a letter.

I haven't done anything about a room for you yet as the Cunninghams are out of town but they will be home by the end of the week. I hope I can have some money for both of us so that you can eat next week but be prepared to starve.

The furniture situation looks encouraging. It now appears that we shall have beds by the first of August and everything else we need by the first of September.

If you want to write letters I would suggest the Illinois Steel Company, 208 S. La Salle St, Chicago, Ill., (perhaps mentioning the recently completed business survey). You might also try Halsey, Stuart & Co. 209 S. LaSalle St., Kemper Insurance Co. 4750 Sheridan Rd. (this is the company that looks over Illinois Life), Harris Trust & Savings Bank, 105 W. Monroe St. Another suggestion would be to try the personnel departments of the large department stores, Marshall, Field & Co., Mandel Brothers and Carson, Pirie, Scott & Co., with the emphasis on your personnel rather than statistical experience. R.R. Donnelly & Sons Co., 350 E. 22nd St. is the biggest publishing and printing house here and might be worth a try. Don't be discouraged by replies telling you there's no work. The fact that you get replies at all impresses me and a reply such as the one you got from the Federal Reserve Bank at least paves the way for a possible job resulting from a personal interview. I just thought of two more. Standard Oil Co. of Indiana, 910 S. Michigan Ave. and International Harvester Co., 606 S. Michigan Ave. I'll have to stop now to tell you I love you - whether you ever write another letter or not, except to me.

Bob

133. Milwaukee, Tuesday [June 27, 1933]

Dear Bob –

If you still want me to take Monday off I can do it and I think it's a great idea. I wasn't smart enough to think of it by myself, but the plan is this. I can take one day of my vacation then and one less in August. My vacation should start Friday, August 11th, because the month ends on Friday, and I can simply start it on Saturday instead, and I won't even have to sacrifice a weekend.

The only trouble is that I haven't a place to stay and I do hate to impose on people, so you write immediately if you think it's a practical idea, and I shall make the final arrangements. I can take it if you tell me that it can't be arranged, but it would be swell to be with you, and I might even get some business done.

I had dinner at the Cooleys tonight. They, too, think you're a personable young man and Margaret is delighted that you like Joe. Some people don't so that makes her feel that you are of the discriminating few.

The heat is getting me down. If I had a dollar I'd write you on it.

There is a clipping in the paper that I wanted to send you but I haven't it at hand. The theme is that honeymoons should be abolished, and that if the truth were known they are excruciating experiences to both parties because circumstances are artificial, travel is annoying and privacy is impossible. Most marriages would be better initiated in the permanent home under normal conditions, say a man and woman writer. I'm inclined to think they may be right so let's save our money for a time when we can take a trip under easier conditions. This is merely a suggestion, of course.

I love you in spite of the weather and my spasmodic attacks of hay fever.

Don't forget to write me about the weekend. I'll expect a letter Thursday.

Betty

P.S. Please, if I come, may we look at rings even if we can't buy them? I know your intentions are honorable but it will be a good opportunity, don't you think?

134. Milwaukee, Wednesday [June 28, 1933]

Dear Bob –

I thought I didn't have anything to write you about but your letter was so inspiring that I have.

I'll try to find out the Cooleys' address before I mail this.

I wrote yesterday to the Household Finance Corporation and to Marshall Field and was about to try the other department stores. You're probably right about the emphasis, but personnel work is a dead field right now though perhaps not more so than statistical work. I told them I was interested in getting selling experience because I think that's about all they hire people for in department stores right now.

I am impressed with your list and I shall get right to work on it.

It has occurred to me that if Stewart is going to be away I might be able to stay in his room at the Plaza. I am still hoping that you can find a place so that I can spend the four days with you, but of course spending money is out of the question.

I am prepared to starve so don't worry about it. I lost my street car pass this morning so I'll starve one day sooner. Everyone seems to think we'll get paid between the fourth and tenth, and if I can get the five bucks from Edris that will keep me until then.

I'm glad to hear about the furniture. That's a break and we are certainly due for one.

I love you very much.

Betty

Mrs. R.L. Cooley

3132 N. Shepard Ave.

135. Chicago, [Wednesday June 28, 1933?]

Dear Betty,

I have made arrangements for you to sleep on the Cunninghams' couch – I even have the key to the apartment – so don't hesitate about getting Monday off. Maybe I can fill the day with business appointments for you.

We shall certainly look at rings and if you doubt my intentions look at the enclosed certificate that I obtained from the marriage license clerk today. Don't fill it in or do anything about it until you see me because it may be simpler for you to obtain the license as an Illinois resident. In any event we both have to appear at the license bureau in person.

I love you enough to marry you even though you are in a state that requires a lot of silly notices, affidavits and examinations.

Bob

136. Milwaukee, Thursday [June 29, 1933]

Dear Bob -

I'm delighted that you'll let me come to see you over the fourth, and I'm even more delighted by receiving the license blank. I'll bring it with me because I don't see how you can establish me as an Illinois resident unless you plan to keep me there unmarried for about six months. I'm amazed that you have to have a physical examination just because I live in Wisconsin, but I'm glad you're willing to overlook even that in me.

I wrote two letters last night and two today. I hope to be somewhere near the end of the list by the time I see you, so you'd better start thinking again.

I wish you would fill Monday with appointments for me. I'd like to see that man at the Federal Reserve Bank between 8:30 and 9, and I suppose I ought to try to see Mr. Pugh. The rest you can arrange for me if you feel so inclined.

I got a reply from McGraw-Hill, the usual one, stating they would keep my application on file. That makes a total of three replies to the three letters I sent last week, which I think is very good, perfect in fact.

I shall arrive on Saturday at the usual time, 2:53. If you want me to meet you someplace else, let me know.

I don't know why I fill my letters so full of business, but I am earnest about it. I love you so much that I have great confidence in my ability to find something in a few months' time, simply because I want it so much for both of us.

May I repeat - I love you.

Betty

137. Chicago, [Wednesday] July 5, 1933 [sent Special Delivery]

Dear Betty,

Last night's confession about my finances must have been very discouraging for you. The failure to keep my bank balance above the level of the receivership funds will be remedied this week as I am depositing more than the deficiency this week and will separate them from my personal account hereafter but the sad fact remains that your intended has at the present time total cash resources of his own of about twenty-five dollars, which is a shameful situation for one who is about to be married to be in. I confidently expect to swell the equity to about a hundred dollars by the end of the month but even that is nothing to cheer over.

I'm afraid you were too decent about your disillusionment and you did make me feel as though I can get over the financial hurdle but my confidence must be small consolation to you. Anyway I love you and I'm going to marry you and it's not going to be done on anybody's money but mine.

Bob

138. Milwaukee, Wednesday [July 5, 1933]

Dear Bob –

I saw Margaret today and she assured me that you could stay at their house if you wished to come up Saturday. You don't have to come nor do you have to stay there if you do, but I thought I'd mention it to you.

Don't forget to write to Mrs. Cooley and please give me the Cunningham's address so I can write to them.

This was one of the nicest weekends I've had with you, much more satisfactory than the short variety. I do love you more the longer I'm with you which makes me delightfully sure that I want to spend my life with you. You can be sure that I'll do everything I can to prove to you that we're doing the right thing by getting married now. I honestly think we'll get along all right. I'm even confident that I'll be able to bring you a dowry of a sort. Whatever happens to us I know that I'll be happy with you and that I'll continue to love you.

We got a letter from Mary today in the office and she says she's very happy doing the washing and the cooking.

I learned today that the girl who was so casual about her wedding day and arrangements has been married for a year. I still think dignity is a nice thing. I don't think, however, that I'll have time to get to the bridesmaids and white veil stage before you marry me.

I'm a selfish little brat and I do burden you too much with my worries but I love you more than I ever expect to love anyone else in my life, not excepting our six children.

Betty

139. Milwaukee, Thursday [July 6, 1933]

Dear Bob -

I just got your letter which almost broke my heart. Darling, please don't feel that I was discouraged or disappointed. You don't seem to realize that I love you and that the amount of money you have is not of any importance as regards my opinion of you. In fact I love you more when I know that you're having a hard time and working so hard and for me - I think it's for me. But why does it hurt you so much to tell me? You mustn't be so proud about those things or you're going to make it very difficult for us when we're married. It's natural I know for you to want to have money when we're about to get married but you must never feel ashamed of not having it. I know that you're doing everything in the world that you can. Please don't ever forget that this is a cooperative enterprise even if you are a man and I'm a woman.

You've made me cry and making me late for work, not because you have twenty-five dollars, sweetheart, but because it has tortured you so to tell me.

Your confession has not shaken my confidence nor my love one infinitesimal bit. I only hope that you'll reach the point when you want to confide your troubles, financial and otherwise to me, because I'm the one to receive them.

Betty

140. Milwaukee, Thursday [July 6, 1933]

Dear Llewellyn -

The name is a term of endearment, not of formality.

I received a letter from Mr. Pugh today. The work has been taken over by a newly organized book company. They will pay one cent a word for manuscripts the amount for one not to exceed fifty dollars, and this will be paid out of royalties and not in advance. He wants me to reply at once in which case he will send me a contract and a new outline for the pamphlets.

I have decided to write him to send them and then have you inspect the contract before I sign it. The catch would seem to be the delay in pay, and also I assume there will be nothing unless the things sell. However, I'm still relying on your judgment so that I may have an alibi in case the project does not pay.

I also received a letter from the Kemper Insurance Company enclosing an application blank and inviting me to call when in Chicago, though they advise me not to make a special trip because they have nothing now. That is rather encouraging, I think.

I hope my letter this morning was not too hysterical but I can't let you act as though your bank balance affects my opinion of your character or ability.

I think we have had quite enough discussion of finances for the present but I must bring up mine for the moment. There seems to be no doubt that we will get paid Monday - there was a formal announcement in the paper today - so if you are planning to come Sunday and are able to support me on that day and perhaps lend me a buck, I wish you'd call Edris and tell her to let the five go until her pay day.[112] I know that she'll have to borrow to get it this week and I hate to press her when she's been so nice to me, so use your judgment and call her if you think it's advisable.

I personally feel that all is well and that we have nothing more to worry about than we have had, perhaps less.

---

[112] An article in the *Milwaukee Journal* for Thursday, July 6, 1933, titled "City's Payroll Cash Growing" with the subtitle, "Employes [*sic*] May Receive May and Part of June Wages, Besides April's," reads: "Payless for more than three months, 11,000 city employes received with enthusiasm Wednesday the news that the April payroll of $1,600,000 would be given to them in cash starting Monday." It adds in the final paragraph: "It is expected that the June salaries will be paid part in cash and part in baby bonds." See n. 105 and n.120.

If it's not too much trouble bring "Painted Veils" with you this weekend. I need something to read.[113]

Come whenever you can. You know it can't be too soon for me. I'm spoiled by having been with you for four days. I want you within arm's reach every minute.

I love you,

Betty

141. Milwaukee, Sunday [July 9, 1933]

Dear Bob -

I thought I would go home and have a good cry over my imaginary and indefinable troubles but Margaret and Joe jarred me into a cheerful mood. We saw a remarkable sight on the way home, a girl playing tennis in white shorts and a flesh colored jersey giving the impression that she was entirely nude above the waist. I'm sorry you missed it. It's the sort of thing you enjoy. Margaret and Joe just fell down the stairs from the third to the second floor in a remarkably comic manner so I'm happy again. All I needed was to see someone get hurt or nearly hurt.

I'm truly sorry that I spoiled what was otherwise a flawless day by being so childish. If I do it again without my slight excuse of today you may beat me. Under the circumstances just try to bear with me because it is a temporary thing.

You are perfect in the sense of being the perfect companion and I confidently expect the perfect husband for me, and I can say that even when I'm in a calm mood.

Nothing you have said to me touched me or thrilled me quite so much as your saying that you lean on me or that you want to. I wish that you would stop being afraid to show me that you do, because I want so desperately to help you, and your surface assurance and self-reliance is so perfect that sometimes it seems to me that I just imagine that I'm any help to

---

113 *Painted Veils* by James Huneker (New York: Liveright Inc. Publishers, 1920) is a lusty tale of society life in New York City between 1880 and 1900, republished in 2005 by Kessinger Publishing. Though Betty clearly used the plural and no article, it is possible that she is referring to *The Painted Veil* by Somerset Maugham, which appeared in 1925.

you at all, that you don't really need me as I need you. That's the surest way to create some character in me, too. Stop bearing all the burdens yourself and perhaps I'll grow up.

What I was trying to convey to you when we were talking in my room was that if a month or so's delay will make the financial situation any easier for you I shall be glad to wait. Aside from that I see no reason for doing so. I should hate, however, to use up any money I may have when I might be with you. What I mean is that living together would be somewhat cheaper and would also give me an opportunity for job hunting which I feel is important not to delay any further. However, if you can possibly manage it I think the wise thing is to get married as soon as possible. In a few more days I should know what money I will have, which is an important part in my decision, whether it is in yours or not. I can't seem to bring up the money situation without your either being evasive or becoming hurt which is one reason why I seem so indecisive. I don't know when you can afford to buy a ring or bear the other expenses incidental to our marriage. Please don't think I'm trying to blame you or to justify myself. I'm simply trying to talk to you as I can't seem to when you're here. I shall try to decide when and where I want to be married within the next week, but my passing the buck is partly due to the fact that I never feel that I have the full information before me on which to make a decision. I suppose that shouldn't concern me at this point. I should decide and let you agree or disagree.

You have given me much more confidence in myself than I ever had before. I hope that I am doing the same for you and that you realize how complete my admiration for you and my faith in you is. I am more fully convinced each day of your intelligence, charm, and sterling worth. In short, I love you.

Betty

142. Milwaukee, Monday [July 10, 1933]

Dear Bob –

I wrote today to True Kimball and to the International Harvester Company. I have no one left to write to except you. Please send me some more names if you can because Verna is on vacation and I have full use of the typewriter now. I'm going to try to find out about civil service examinations in Chicago but that's a slim hope.

I have just finished reading "British Agent" and am consequently suffering from the delusion that we are beleaguered in separate prisons and that our chances of escape or successful communication are very slight. If you should receive this letter please send supplies at once. Incidentally you ought to read the book. It's excellent. Doris seems to buy them and dislike them, while I borrow them and enjoy them.[114]

I saw my pay check today and will get it and deposit it tomorrow. It was all I could do to keep myself from clutching it, but I knew it would be safer there than in my hands until the bank opens.[115]

I was very much impressed by your quickness in the True Kimball situation. It looks like a really good lead. As I have always said, with two such intelligent people working on the problem, how can we fail?

I miss you and love you. I hope the next four days won't be as long as they seem now. Let's have fun and get our teeth cleaned or something. Or let's invite Drs. Bissell and Rice-Wray to dinner and have a physical examination in return.

I really do love you.

Betty

143. Milwaukee, Tuesday [July 11, 1933]

Dear Bob -

I am enclosing a copy of the contract which Mr. Pugh sent me. If you don't mind I'd like to have you look it over and return it immediately with your considered opinion so that I may write him. He doesn't mention the one I have turned in, so I don't know how to assure myself of the profits, if any, arising from that. I'm sure you'll have the same opinion you expressed

---

114 *British Agent* by R. H. Bruce Lockhart, was published by G. P. Putnam's Sons, New York and London, in February 1933. It is a spy thriller based on the author's own experience as a British agent during the Communist takeover in Russia.

115 The *Milwaukee Journal* for Monday, July 10, 1933, has a photo and caption "Payday for City Employes [sic], Including Teachers" with a short notice: "It was July 10 but it was April payday Monday for 11,000 city employes. The upper picture shows employes crowding into the city treasurer's office at the city hall to sign the payroll. There was also a jam at the school board headquarters."

last weekend, but surely I may ask your legal advice, even if I must make my decisions on other matters.

I got a note from Edris today with the five dollars which made me feel very bad, but there's no use telling her now that I could have waited, so I'm keeping it.

I'm going to try to arrange next weekend for a physical examination and operation the following weekend. I don't see how I can make an appointment from here, so it looks as though our marriage won't be the 21st or 22nd. However, I'm going to do all the planning and make all the preparations I can so that you won't be stopped the next time you suggest a date. I'll discuss it with you further next weekend, but I thought you might like to know the results thus far of my tangled thinking.

I love you very much and I want you and need you. I'll be very glad when all this unsettled situation is cleared up and I know that you will be even more so. I'm really doing my best now so just relax and before you know it I'll be telling you where to present yourself. That last statement is supposed to cheer you; it may depress you instead. Anyway, I love you.

Betty

P.S. Don't forget the contract. He's in a panic to have it returned and I'll feel better when I've written him the final decision.

144. Chicago, [Wednesday, July 12, 1933]

Dear Betty,

I have even run out of business stationery. This is the kind I had when I first began practicing and you can see how far I have advanced.

I hope to h -- what I hoped to have I apparently forgot while I was tracing the Hawkins & Lo you see before you.[116] I think it had something to do with marriage. Anyway I hope to have your ring by the 21st so that we can get married that week end if it seems advisable.

I told you what the financial situation was but rather than know it I suppose you prefer not to believe me. If you will remind me I will give you a detailed statement as of July 15, this week end but that won't tell you what it

---

[116] A large traced HAWKINS & LO is inserted in the body of the letter (see Illustration No. 30). When held to the light, the whole watermark of Hawkins & Loomis Co appears.

will be August 1 or at any other future date. It bothers me just as much as it does you but I can't improve it much staying single and if I could I wouldn't. For your part you are a damn fool to marry me at all but I love you for being that kind of a damn fool, which no doubt results from that 93% emotional sensitivity. Where you are concerned mine is 100.

Bob

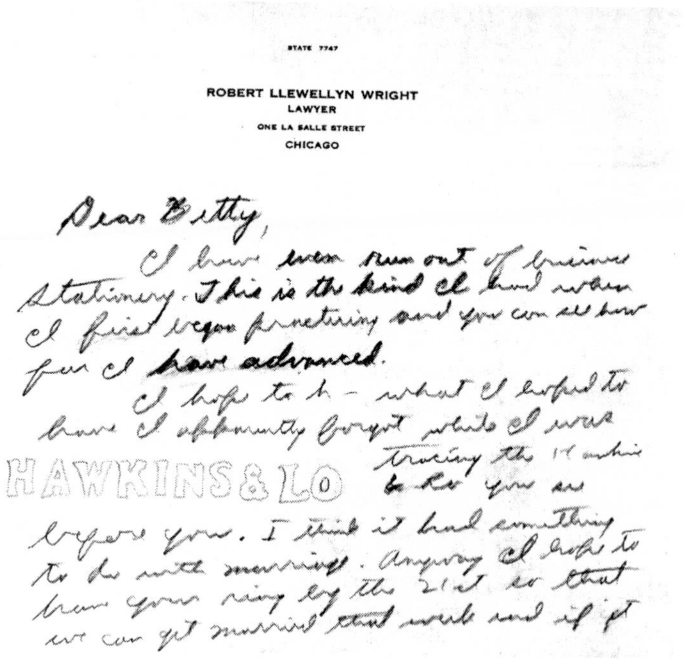

STATE 7747

ROBERT LLEWELLYN WRIGHT
LAWYER
ONE LA SALLE STREET
CHICAGO

Dear Betty,

I have even run out of business stationery. This is the kind I had when I first began practicing and you can see how far I have advanced.

I hope to h— what I hoped to have I apparently forgot while I was tracing the [illegible] [illegible] you as

HAWKINS & LO

before you. I think it had something to do with marriage. Anyway I hope to have your ring by the 21st so that we can get married that week and if [illegible]

30. *Letter No. 144, with old letterhead and tracing*

Part Five: The Wedding Is On!

Letters 145-157, July 12-27, 1933

145. Milwaukee, Wednesday [July 12, 1933]

Dear Llewellyn -

I hope you find some envelopes soon, for although I got an immense thrill out of your telegram, I find that on the tenth reading they pall as your letters do not. I realized today how lucky I am, however, when I met a girl whose fiancé is in Singapore and it takes her a month to get his letters. What would I do with all my little problems in a case like that?

While I still don't quite see how we can get married the week after next I'm willing to exert every effort to do so. I shopped for wedding announcements today and got some very good prices. Do you suppose you could make out a list with addresses soon? Maybe your mother would do it for you. I'll have to know how many to order and the addressing is a big job. I have a feeling you won't need one hundred and fifty for yourself but you certainly may have them if you do. My list to date totals about thirty-five, though I have probably left out many, and I have included none of your friends in Chicago.

Today marks a lift in the great depression of Elizabeth Bryan Kehler. I had begun to think that the rest of my life would be spent on the verge of tears. It's a swell feeling, and I love you with renewed vigor.

Your father spoke in Milwaukee yesterday at the Normal School at the solicitation of Dr. Joseph Klotschi. Margaret rushed in from Oostberg to hear him and she said that his lecture was not only understandable but the best sermon she had heard in years. I wish that I might have heard him. She thinks you look like him.[117]

---

[117] The *Milwaukee Journal* for Tuesday, July 11, 1933, reports on this lecture in an article titled "All Wrong to Wright, Courthouse Above All" that begins: "Modern education, civilization, culture,

It seems to me only right and proper to invite my mother to our wedding though I'm sure she won't come. Don't you think you ought to invite yours?

I love you, darling, more and more. I'm not a bit afraid to marry you, though if it were anyone else I would have to consider it carefully. How could I fail to love you when you're everything I've always wanted?

Betty

146. Milwaukee, Thursday [July 13, 1933]

Dear Bob -

Probably the nicest thing about you is your financial situation and the fact that you're willing to marry me in spite of it. What would I do if you were one of these guys who value their standard of living more than a mate? I'd go crazy wanting you, is the answer. Don't be too concerned over my inquiries. I get that way occasionally but it doesn't last. That will be solved anyway when I become the family accountant.

I haven't much to report except that I'll see you Saturday at the usual place and time if you don't object. I wrote a note to Edris and if she gives you the name of a doctor take it and don't argue.

I love you and I hope we can get married within the next two weeks. I love you -

Betty

P.S. You'd better get some more of that swell stationery. I don't care about myself but I won't have you conducting business on this plebeian stuff.

147. Chicago, [Monday, July 17, 1933]

Dear Betty,

Enclosed is Mr. Pugh's contract.[118] Write him as follows:

---

capitalism, houses, clothes manners, and mental concepts—all fail to express the soul or any inner essential truth, Frank Lloyd Wright, the world famous architect of Spring Green, Wis., said in a talk Tuesday morning before the assembly of the state teachers' college." It continues in the third and fourth paragraphs to relate Wright's strong criticism of the new Milwaukee courthouse building.

[118] The actual contract is found as an enclosure with the letter. See Illustration No. 32.

"I am returning unsigned herewith the contract dated July 10, 1933 with the Commonwealth Book Company, as I can not afford to spend the time necessary to produce the pamphlets without definite assurance of receiving compensation for them.

Please let me know what has been done with the pamphlet I submitted. My understanding with respect to this particular pamphlet is that I am to receive a 6% royalty on its gross sales. If it has been published I should like to know what if any sale has been made."

That will teach him to take advantage of a young girl in a public library.

There I go again, day-dreaming.[119]

If I'm going to get any work done I'll have to just tell you I love you and cease writing.

Bob

---

[119] A large doodle is represented after this sentence—a double pointed pencil? See Illustration No. 31.

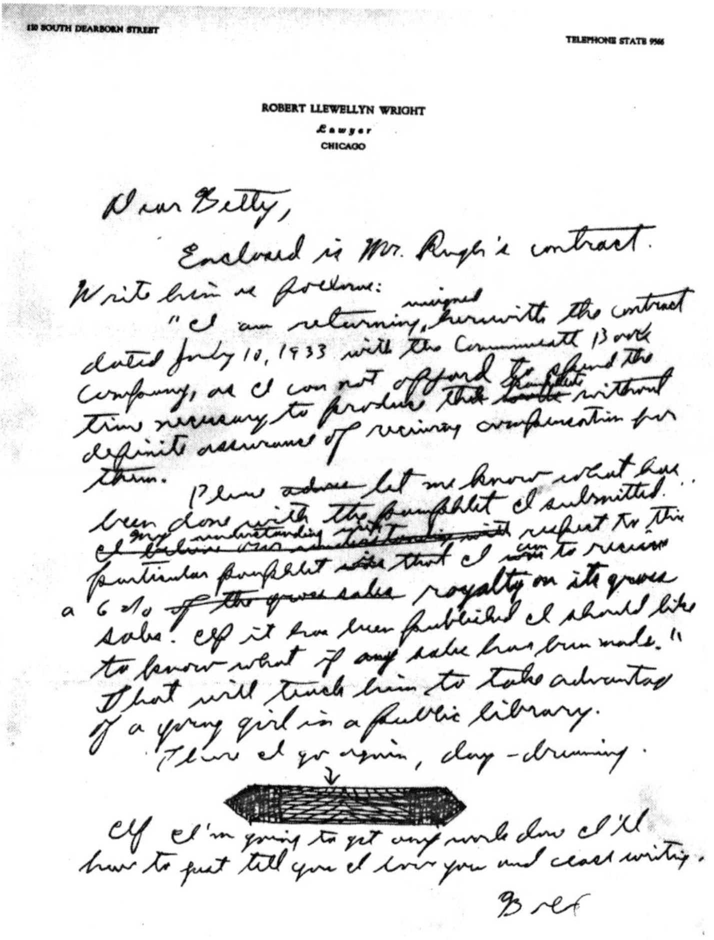

110 SOUTH DEARBORN STREET

TELEPHONE STATE 9566

ROBERT LLEWELLYN WRIGHT
Lawyer
CHICAGO

Dear Betty,

Enclosed is Mr. Rugh's contract. Write him as follows:

"I am returning signed herewith the contract dated July 10, 1933 with the Commonwealth Book Company, as I can not afford to spend the time necessary to produce without definite assurance of receiving compensation for them.

Please let me know what has been done with the pamphlet I submitted. My understanding with respect to this particular pamphlet is that I am to receive a 6% royalty on its gross sales. If it has been published I should like to know what if any sales has been made."

That will teach him to take advantage of a young girl in a public library.

There I go again, day-dreaming.

If I'm going to get any work done I'll have to just tell you I love you and cease writing.

Bob

31. *Letter No. 147, with doodle*

THIS AGREEMENT, made and entered into in duplicate this 10th day of ~~June~~ July, 1933, by and between COMMONWEALTH BOOK COMPANY, a corporation organized under the laws of the State of Illinois, with its principal place of business in the City of Chicago, Illinois, hereinafter designated as party of the first part, and Elizabeth B. Keller, of the City of ~~Chicago, Illinois~~ Milwaukee, Wisconsin, hereinafter designated as party of the second part,

WITNESSETH: that

The party of the second part hereby agrees to write and prepare for the party of the first part a series of manuscripts on Vocational Guidance subjects to be mutually agreed upon, and do make printed booklets of not less than sixteen (16) and not more than thirty-two (32) pages, type sizes about 6¼ x 9¼ inches of 12 pt. type, said manuscripts to first be approved by Miss Ann Davis, Vocational Guidance Editor for the party of the first part, or, in case of her inability to act in such capacity, any other editor selected for the purpose by the party of the first part. The party of the second part agrees to make such revisions as said editor or the party of the first part may deem necessary and to furnish a suitable copy of said manuscripts with such revisions, if necessary, and in shape to submit to the compositor.

It is expressly understood that said manuscripts shall be and remain the property of the party of the first part, and that copyright shall be taken out in the name of said party of the first part; further, the party of the second part represents and agrees that all such material is and shall be original matter gathered and compiled from reliable sources, and that no other person, persons or company has any right, interest or title in the same, and that said material in no way infringes upon any copyright.

In consideration of the foregoing the party of the first part hereby agrees to publish such manuscripts, approved and accepted by said party of the first part, in a good and workmanlike manner, and to offer the same for sale to the best of its ability, both through the mail and through agents in the field, and to pay said party of the second part, his or her heirs or assigns, one cent (1¢) per word (exclusive of "a," "an," "and," "the," and "but"), but not more than fifty dollars ($50) for any one manuscript, said payment to be made out of the sales of said published manuscript at the rate ofnot less than ten per cent (10% of the money received by the party of the first part from the sales of the same within any one year. Settlement of amounts due hereunder shall be made once each year on the first day of April beginning April 1, 1934, until said amount has been paid in full.

IN WITNESS WHEREOF, both parties have hereunto affixed their signatures, the day and date first above written.

COMMONWEALTH BOOK COMPANY

By ______________________
Vice President.

Witnesses: ______________________ (SEAL)

____

____

32. Contract enclosed with Letter No. 147

148. Milwaukee, Monday [July 17, 1933]

Dear Bob –

The engraving company says that while they could start the plate it would save little time. The important thing is to get the order in so that they have the paper and envelopes on hand, which means that the next thing for us is to decide on the number we want. They also promise to get them out on two or three days' notice if necessary.

I went to one shop today to look at dresses and while I didn't find exactly what I want I was delighted by the good looking things they had at amazingly low prices. I think I'll buy a dozen while I'm about it. This is a swell time to buy. (I'm fooling about the dozen, please note)

There was an article in the paper stating that we might get another month's pay by the end of the week. In fact, the atmosphere in which I move is charged with optimism and I feel that the world is a beautiful place.[120]

I have just been invited to the Cooleys so I'll have to hurry. I love you so much, my darling, that there's no sense in trying to tell you about it. You'll just have to feel it. I'm very happy about our approaching marriage – in fact I'm ecstatic and I want everyone to be there. I can't wait for the time when I won't have to leave you ever again – I love everything about you –

Betty

149. Milwaukee, Tuesday [July 18, 1933]

Dear Bob –

Thank you for the letter. I had already written Mr. Pugh but I wrote him to the same effect. Nevertheless the letter wasn't wasted because I know that on Monday you still loved me.

---

[120] The *Milwaukee Journal* for Monday, July 17, 1933, has an article titled "Payday May Come Soon Again for City Workers," which reads: "It is probable that there will be another payday for city employes the latter part of this week, Treasurer J. W. Murdoch announced Monday..... The treasurer at the close of business Monday expected to have enough to meet an entire month's payroll, but he was not sure whether he would pay employes completely for the month of May. If the proposal to give city employes 25 per cent of their salaries in baby bonds is accepted by the [common council's finance] committee it is probable that they will be paid for the entire month." See n. 105 and n. 112 above.

I have been shopping assiduously without spending a cent so far. That's the way I intend to shop after I'm married.

Please don't think that you have to come here on my birthday. It was sweet of you to think of it at all, but it's not necessary because I'll see you the very next day and I know that you love me as I love you. I may have put undue emphasis on it with my plans to come down there on Friday but it really isn't important to me at all.

How can I wait these four long weeks when I love you so much?

Betty

150. Chicago, [Wednesday] 7/19/33

Dear Betty,

I made an appointment for a physical examination tomorrow and tonight I shall call Mother about the list so you see the wedding preparations are taking up almost as much of my time as yours, although I am not buying a suit to get married in and we shall have to rely on your dress for the necessary novelty touch.

I had lunch with Stewart yesterday. He wanted us to come out to Lake Forest some week-end but I told him we might be married week after next and even went so far as to invite him and Nell to the wedding. He said he had a birthday present for you which is more than I've got.

The ring is the next thing on the list but I want to order it so that it will be delivered just before we get married, thus preventing me from losing it and thereby losing you.

Bob

151. Chicago, [Thursday] July 20, 1933

Dear Betty,

The ring is ordered but won't be ready till next Tuesday. For your birthday I have decided to make you a present of a negative Wasserman test, that is, the gratifying news supplied by the test that I am not afflicted with a venereal disease. This should make you just as happy as Margaret's mother was when she learned her daughter was not afflicted with a chancre. I was scheduled for an examination by Dr. Riba this morning but forgot the appointment, and hope to keep one tomorrow.

I'm afraid I can't get to Milwaukee for your birthday as I had hoped but will see you Saturday anyway. There is a present from Stewart and Nell waiting for you.

Love, Bob

152. Milwaukee, Thursday [July 20, 1933]

Dear Bob -

I am impressed by all your preparations, though you rather worry me about the ring. What if it shouldn't be ready in time? However, that's your responsibility and having mentioned it I shall cease to worry.

I haven't bought a dress yet though I have been looking hard. I want to look beautiful and I'm afraid it makes me too critical. I'll find something, I suppose. I bought a bathing suit and cap yesterday so you'll have to take me swimming before the summer is over. It's blue and it hasn't any back. I hope you'll like it.

I received a letter from Mother today saying that she didn't feel able to come to the wedding. It made me feel very sad. I really wish she could come. She enclosed a check for fifty dollars which she said was a wedding present which she thought I might need now. That isn't fair because it's rightfully ours, not mine. I was shocked to see it and I don't know whether I ought to keep it or not. I never saw the day when my family had fifty dollars all at once. What do you think I ought to do? She wrote me a very sweet letter and I think she loves me. That makes two who do, though you forgot to mention it.

I had a half holiday yesterday for Milwaukee's Homecoming or something. I was very much surprised. I went on a picnic with Danny and some other people and I got a skinned knee, a blistered finger and a terrific case of hay fever. Can't you stop me from going on beach picnics? I told you I didn't like them.

Your letters are so brief. I suppose it's because you're busy trying to marry me. Don't let it get you down. If we can't get married the 29th we'll get married some other time. It's a marriage of convenience anyway, you know. Please don't let it stop you from being affectionate.

I love you, sweetheart.

Betty

[written up the side of the page] P.S. What do you mean you haven't a birthday present for me? You've already given me one, and you're going to give me several more in a few weeks. Again I must say I love you – E.

153. Milwaukee, Monday [July 24, 1933]

Dear Bob –

I pulled myself together sufficiently to buy a dress today. It's tan. I hope you'll like it. I look like the same old girl in it, instead of as I had hoped, the astoundingly beautiful Mrs. Wright, but I can't expect you to change my face as well as my character.

I find that the only address I have not obtained is that of Coke and Julia.[121] Could you get it from the Carsons or Stewart? The announcements are ordered but I can't have the envelopes until Wednesday so the last two days will be somewhat crowded.

I bought the douce [douche] business today. Although I tried to approach the clerk with the utmost aplomb, my lack of knowledge of the terminology was so apparent that I became confused. I'll be glad when I'm a married woman instead of a blushing maiden.

I think I'll make the grade all right so you don't have to worry about me any more.

I am glad for one reason that I had the small medical difficulty this weekend because it gave me further knowledge of how perfect you are. I can't tell you how much it means to me to know that you will be patient, understanding and optimistic no matter what problems we have. It gives me such a wonderfully sure conviction that you love me as I want to be loved and as I want to love you.

Just one more suggestion. I think you ought to find out soon whether your mother can come at eleven and if she can't try to postpone it for an hour or so. I really think she ought to be there.

I love you –

Betty

---

[121] Julia was Keith Ransom's daughter by her first marriage (See "Introduction" and Illustration No. 10), and Coke Miller was Julia's first husband.

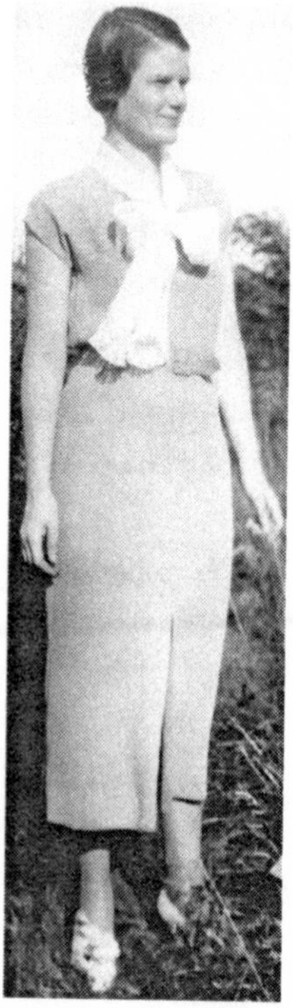

33. Betty in her wedding dress

154. Chicago, [Tuesday] 7/25/33

Dear Betty,

Here is another announcement envelope for you to address.

Mr. & Mrs. Follett W. Bull

Miss Helen Bull

300 N. Grove Ave., Oak Park, Ill.

I hope that you are keeping spiritually fit so that you may survive Mr. Hume's most rigid test. I am of course devoting this week to meditation and silent prayer.

However, I am going to risk ruining the pious atmosphere with which we have been surrounded by telling again that I love you, not merely with a religious fervor, but with certain elements of bodily lust, which I will of course keep under control as much as possible. I can't believe yet that we're actually on the point of marrying but rather suspect that the trick will have been painlessly accomplished by Saturday noon.

Love, Bob[122]

155. Chicago, [Wednesday] 7/26/33

Dear Betty,

The Miller's address is 732 Ferry St., Buffalo, N.Y. I have communicated with all the proposed wedding guests and a record attendance is assured. Dave will bring mother and Stewart is reluctantly taking time off from work. He says why don't we get married in the afternoon like other people but I refused to change the hour. I told him that we would like to have Nell too but if she has to make a special trip from Lake Forest and would rather not go to the trouble there will be no hurt feelings. Incidentally, have you thanked them for your birthday present?

I have the ring and about the only thing left is our spiritual preparation by Mr. Hume. I shall call him Friday to make the appointment for 9:30. It just occurred to me that you would need some flowers. Please let me know at once what you require so that if we have to send away for some rare specimens we can get them.

Love, Bob

156. Milwaukee, [Thursday] July 27, 1933

Dear Bob –

Thank you for the letter. Though I have neglected you I have been thinking about you as well as about myself.

---

[122] On July 25, 1933, Llewellyn sent a letter to his father inviting him to the wedding at eleven o'clock Saturday morning July 29 at the New England Congregational Church, Delaware Place and Dearborn St. He said the ceremony would be "a simple one…with only members of the family in attendance.… There will be no reception or trimmings of any sort, and if I have my way, the whole affair will be run off in about twenty-minutes, so you won't be detained long if you appear." He also asks his father to invite his sister Frances if she is planning to be in Chicago at that time (WO71D05, Frank Lloyd Wright Archive, copyright @ The Frank Lloyd Wright Foundation 1990).

I addressed and stamped all the envelopes last night. Tonight I'll have to insert the announcements and seal them. The paper is very nice. I have addressed them to all the names we have, including the doubtful ones, and I have five left over, so hold your last minute inspirations down to that number.

It seems to me that Saturday will never come. I can't imagine being scared even at the last minute, because I love you and want to marry you so much.

Betty

157. Milwaukee, Thursday [July 27, 1933]

Dear Bob -

I had counted on your forgetting flowers and consequently would not have been disappointed. I do think they would be a nice thing, however. A small white shoulder corsage would be nice, I think, nothing large or elaborate. The only white flowers I can think of are gardenias which I like very much. If you prefer something else it's all right.

I haven't written Nell because I haven't any personal stationery. Is that awful?

I love you and I'll see you tomorrow at 6:53, Grand Avenue.

Betty

Part Six: Married

The Dream Becomes Real

Letters 158–168, July 31–August 10, 1933

158. Milwaukee, Monday [July 31, 1933]

My darling –

Now that I'm back here I can hardly believe it's really true – it seems so much like a beautiful dream. I won't try to tell you how I feel about you because those things are better left unexpressed -- I know you understand. But as you said, if we never have anything more than this one weekend our marriage has been worthwhile.

As I got off the train this morning Mrs. Howard Simmons who was on the same train rushed up from behind me to offer me her best wishes and tell me she had gotten the announcement this morning and had noticed me just as I stood up. I was in an utter fog and I'm afraid my reactions were pretty dumb. I couldn't think who she was for quite some time. She had been down to the pigeon festival and was returning to Oconomowoc.

I sneaked into the office about noon. Van was the only one there and he was awfully nice. He didn't tease me at all until later in the afternoon when I had had some food and gotten my bearings somewhat, and then in a way I didn't mind. Mr. Winkel was disappointing. He was too shy about it all to utter his best platitudes.

My impression is that Stewart's address is 925 Lake Drive. I shall probably not write until tomorrow but if that isn't it you might call Stewart later in the week to see if they received the letter.

Prepare yourself to convince me next weekend that I have really married you. I won't believe it until I'm with you again.

Love, Betty

P.S. I couldn't resist writing my name on the back. It's too bad you haven't a new title. You'll never know how silly and excited and happy it makes me feel.[123]

159. Chicago, [Tuesday] 8/1/33 [sent Special Delivery][124]

Dear Betty,

I just caught myself biting my nails. Maybe marriage hasn't changed me any more than it has you. But if it never changes you I'll be more than satisfied.

You made the week-end exceed all my expectations and when you were able to do that under unfavorable climactic conditions think what wonders you will accomplish in the basement. Remember, too, that the Fall is coming and you are not yet really at your best.

I feel now as though I were just beginning to love you.

Bob

34. Envelope for Letter No. 159, addressed to Mrs. Elizabeth Kehler Wright, with a Special Delivery stamp and Chicago 1933 World's Fair commemorative stamp

---

[123] Betty has written Mrs. R. L. Wright on the back of the envelope.

[124] The envelope is addressed to Mrs. Elizabeth Kehler Wright. See Illustration No. 34.

160. Milwaukee, Tuesday [August 1, 1933]

Dear Bob –

I'm just fresh from having a wisdom tooth pulled so I'm hastening to write you before I feel worse. It didn't hurt a bit. I feel shaky but I think that's a result of my well-known habit of over anticipating unpleasantness.

I don't see how the weekend could help exceeding your expectations which were pretty black. However I know that you are as happy over it as I am which is saying a great deal.

I wrote Nell today telling her I would be there at 2:18 daylight saving time. Come as soon as you can but no sooner.

You may address me by your name here. They know you.

I love you and I'll be extraordinarily happy to be with you again.

Betty

161. Milwaukee, Wednesday [August 2, 1933]

Dear Bob –

Letters seem more futile than ever, don't they, now that we're married? Nevertheless I still write them and want them.

I find that I have a slightly different reaction toward being without you. I feel more calm, less frustrated but life seems so flat. It's so meaningless to be living this same old life instead of the exciting new one with you. I'm really looking forward to keeping house and attempting to cook for you. I'd like to wait on you hand and foot. I know that I'm still the same imperfect individual and that a ten-minute ceremony won't change me painlessly into a perfect one, but I can't believe that living with you and loving you won't help to make me more nearly as I'd like to be.

What a damned sentimentalist I am! I'll probably make your life miserable.

It's raining tonight – an ideal situation for a cozy evening in the basement. That's the reason I'm mooning around and telling you what a good wife I'm going to be.

I didn't have any trouble with my tooth extraction so I have practically nothing to worry about at present. Can't you think of something?

Write me and tell me what I already know – that you love me as I love you, more than I ever did before. Even with a wedding ring on my finger I still like to hear it.

Betty

162. Chicago, [Thursday] Aug. 3, 1933

Dear Betty,

It seems silly for me to be corresponding with you when we ought to be living together. You are my wife, aren't you? Then what the hell are you doing in Milwaukee? I'm afraid that a two day taste of married life has made me an addict and the separation from you now is harder to bear than it ever was before. That intelligent people advocate voluntary separations for married couples seems at the moment incredible.

Why I should call you "Dear Betty" when we are lovers in fact as well as fancy also puzzles me but "Sweetheart" is inadequate and you've already used "My darling" on me, which thrilled me because I know how hard it was for you to use. I think I'll refer to you simply as my "heart" because I can't really function without you and you're all I have in what passes anatomically for my heart. If I'm not in Lake Forest before you are Saturday it will be because I've broken a leg trying to catch a train.

Bob

163. Milwaukee, Thursday [August 3, 1933]

Dear Bob –

Your letter makes me want to use all the endearing terms in my vocabulary but I don't want to dull your response to them. There are so few of them that mean anything and I want them to mean so much.

I'm glad that we didn't wait a minute longer to get married. Our love seems so much more sure now that the initial uncertainty is over. But at the same time I'm actually glad we weren't married sooner, because it isn't right – it isn't really marriage – to be separated from you now during the week. You are my lover now, which is a big step in the right direction, but you won't be my husband until I'm actually a part of your household and your daily life.

My friend Mrs. Ladwig who is now a widow but who apparently had an unusually successful married life is always shocked and annoyed when young couples spend a great deal of time apart and assert that it is helping their marriage relationship. She says that she and her husband could never understand how time spent without each other meant anything but less time being happy together, which is unanswerable logic, I think, if two people have the intelligence to remain happy with each other. I see no reason why we shouldn't make that our aim.

The girls in the main office most of whom are not girls in the young sense are fascinated by my wedding ring which they think is the 1933 style and "so different". I haven't the heart to tell them that there are some people who buy rings not because they're a current style but because they like them and hope no one else will follow suit. I am growing more fond of it every day. I mentioned that it seems a little large in this cool weather but was assured that my hands will swell as soon as I start doing housework. A nice thought. I love you and I'm glad this is the last day [the rest is written up the side of the page] I'll be writing a letter, for the day after tomorrow I'll be in your arms and in your bed. Rather crude of me but a delightful thought nevertheless –

Betty

164. Milwaukee, Monday [August 7, 1933]

Dear Bob –

I've just written an enormous letter to Mother answering ten thousand questions she asked me, and a note to Nell. I find the last of the stationery gone and I hope you're not hurt. I'll buy some which should last both of us a long time since we won't be writing each other. Would you consent to use the folded variety with a faint stripe I used to write you on, or would you prefer a more masculine type? Be like I am and answer my questions.

If you write me definitely that you are driving here and if I get it packed I may send the trunk earlier in the week. I'm sure you couldn't get it in a car. If you want to try it I'll wait.

I functioned exceptionally well today, placing housemaids like mad. Pat's here but he doesn't bother me. I hope I work for some one just like him in Chicago so that I never have an opportunity to cease to realize how wonderful and remarkable you are among males.

It was very sad to see you cross over to the other side of the tracks and leave in an opposite direction. It almost might have been a bit of movie symbolism except for the fact that we're going to travel in the same direction for the rest of our lives.

I don't understand how I can love you more each week but I do. Because I love you I'm going to will these five days past in no time at all so that I can start cooking your meals and demonstrating my perfect fitness to be your wife.

Love, Betty

165. Chicago, [Tuesday, August 8, 1933][125]

Dear Betty,

I'm afraid we're going to have to break a succession of pleasure week-ends with one of hard work. I will pick-up Dave's car Saturday morning at the plant and arrive in Milwaukee with it between twelve and one. Then we can drive to Chicago Saturday afternoon but we won't drive to Gary till Sunday morning as they will be a bit crowded there Saturday night. This will deprive us of an opportunity to test the beds but I can assure you that they are satisfactory for sleeping and I assume that we will not have occasion to use them for much else this week-end. By the way, how are your breasts?

Anyway, I love you, whether we work or play and am looking forward to spending the night with you at Division St. regardless of your condition. Don't let me forget to carry you across the door-step.

More love,

Bob

[125] The envelope is addressed to Mrs. R. L. Wright at the Milwaukee Vocational School (see Illustration No. 35).

35. Envelope for Letter No. 165, addressed to Mrs. R. L. Wright at the Milwaukee Vocational School, with a stamp commemorating the 1933 Chicago World's Fair, Century of Progress

166. Tuesday, Milwaukee, [August 8, 1933]

Dear Bob –

I think it's a little mean of you not to write me on my tooth extraction days, Tuesday and Thursday, though I imagine I'd love you just as much if you never wrote or if you wrote poison pen letters daily.

I'm a lovely creature. I'm holding ice to the jaw, spitting blood, smoking and writing a letter at the same time. That should at least produce a telegram telling me to stop smoking. The dentist assures me that these will hurt but I haven't experienced it yet so I'm hoping for the best. You may have to spend the weekend doing my packing for me.

I will now stop talking about it because I know you aren't interested anyway.

Margaret came home last night and took me for a ride with her sister and a wayward boy cousin who looks about fifteen, has a six weeks old son and has just arrived via freight cars from Salt Lake City for what purpose I know not. Aside from that I have nothing to report.

I may have mentioned it before, but I do love you. I can hardly wait for you to come and carry me away. You will come, won't you? I'll be such a good girl if you'll just let me live with you –

Betty

167. Milwaukee, Thursday [August 10, 1933; sent Special Delivery]

Dear Bob –

This will be just a note under the watchful eye of Mr. Patterson.[126]

I packed most of my trunk last night and when I finish, I'm going to send it. I would be ridiculous to try to put it in a car.

I'm planning to have the last tooth out tonight and the socket of the preceding one doesn't feel so good. I'm telling you this because I may still have packing to do when you arrive on Saturday and I trust you will be patient with me.

The plan for the weekend sounds great to me. I have been longing for work.

I liked your last letter. My breasts are all right now that I've gotten away from you.

I have very pleasant visions of spending the night at home. Do you remember the last night spent there? I hope this will be different.

I love you with all my heart.

Betty

168. Chicago, [Thursday] 8/10/33 [sent Special Delivery]

Elizabeth Darling

How's that! This is a special aching tooth letter and I feel that I must go the limit to relieve the pain. It is certainly thoughtful of you to have your unpleasant feelings away from me instead of with me and I appreciate it. Not that I expect you to be in perfect physical condition on Saturday but I shall be surprised if I find you spitting blood.

If you haven't already expressed your trunk I suggest that you do so at once. Coming after you and carrying you away, literally, with all your belongings, is a romantic performance that few brides experience. Perhaps Mr. Mills can arrange to offer the necessary resistance by trying to hold you and your baggage for the rent. The effect will not be spoiled by your sending the trunk in advance, however.

---

126 The letter is written on Milwaukee Vocational School stationery.

Saturday I'm going to begin loving you every day in person but until then I can only go through the dull motions of sending it to you.

Bob

Appendix

The following obituary for James Howard Kehler was found in Betty's papers. It must have come from the obituary pages for a Cliff Dwellers publication.

James Howard Kehler

1876–1923

A picturesque figure dropped out of our ranks when James Howard Kehler—Jim to most of us—went to join his ancestors. He had been a vivid personality in the club's life for years; he was a familiar face at the luncheon tables, a well-known voice among our best talkers. The Cliff Dwellers was his steady rendezvous; he was one of The Regulars. At the guest-of-honor noon-day gatherings, the Harvest Home dinners, the annual meetings, the ladies' nights, he could almost always be found among the brotherhood, quietly congenial, pleasantly ironic, seraphically decorative.

To our Chicagoesque plainness he brought a touch of color, for he had a way of looking like a young poet who had decided to go in for archaic dandyism. There was a dash of the *incroyable* in him. But behind that attitude there was power, and keen, bold, free thinking. He caught the attention without clamoring for it, and when he spoke he said something. His views and opinions were often unorthodox, but they were heresies that stimulated. He was distinctly an anti-Babbitt.

His career began in journalism, but soon branched off into advertising, where he became a pathfinder. He brought his work into touch with art and letters. He was one of the first to instruct his profession in the use of lucid, debunked English, good taste, and psychological strategy. He was a power in the development of modern advertising technique and all of his work had the *cachet* of his strong individuality.

He had a wide acquaintance among writers and artists, here and in New York, and he helped many a career on its way. His spirit was emancipated, his impulses generous, his eyes open to signs of promise. There was a strain of genius in Jim Kehler, which expressed itself in several ways; and, what is more important, there was also a great charm and kindliness of soul. He was a creative influence, and his passing in the vigor of his middle age is greatly to be lamented. C.C.

[55–56. P. 55 has the last eight lines of an obituary for Gustav Holmquist. On p. 56, an obituary for Alonzo Kimball, 1874–1923, begins.]

List of Illustrations

The originals of all items were found in Elizabeth Kehler Wright's personal papers. The titles in quotes are her annotations on the back of or below the photos.

1. "James Howard Kehler before I was born." Matted studio photo; Gibson Art Galleries, 195-197 Wabash Ave, Chicago.

2. "Catherine Tobin Wright." Unframed photo.

3. "Elizabeth Osgood Kehler." Matted studio photo.

4. "Will and Bess' Home." Snapshot matted on dark gray construction paper similar to other photos dated 1912. The house (still standing) is 422 Clinton Ave, Oak Park, IL, residence of Wm R Lloyd and Elizabeth Osgood Kehler Lloyd, where Betty lived as a young girl.

5. "Elizabeth Bryan Kehler, Born July 21, 1910, Picture taken summer of 1912." Snapshot. A version of the same snapshot matted on dark grey construction paper is titled "In Aunt Zilpha's backyard, Summer 1912."

6. "Bess Osgood Lloyd, Elizabeth Bryan Kehler." Matted studio photo; Koehne Bush Temple Studios, 800 N. Clark St, Chicago.

7. "Llewellyn Wright at 6, 1909." Matted studio photo; Arnold.

8. "Wm R. Lloyd, Aunt Zilpha Lloyd, Elizabeth Bryan Kehler, and Cousin Annie White." A later addition in Betty's hand says: "& old Ford that turned over once—starting my auto-phobias." Snapshot.

9. Postcard with printed caption "Congregational Church and Parsonage, St. Charles, Minn."

10. "Julia Ransom, Vassar days." Matted studio photo; Wolven, Poughkeepsie.

11. "Property of Bess Osgood Lloyd. Elizabeth Bryan Kehler, April 1931, Graduated from University of Wisconsin June 1931." Matted studio photo; The Longe Studio, Madison.

12. "Betty W—Pregnant, Street Photographer." Snapshot. Natural Moving Picture Co., Oak Park, IL.

13. "Elizabeth K. Wright & Thomas." Studio photo pasted on stiff cardboard.

INDEX

Note: Page references followed by "*p*" refer to photos. Page references followed by "*n*" refer to notes.

C

G

H

L

M

Q

R

S

Y

Z

LaVergne, TN USA
01 June 2010
184608LV00002B/64/P